£1.50

D0518646

Edited by Anthony du Gard Pasley

Allen Lane

Summer Flowers

Illustrations with descriptive text copyright
© Carters Tested Seeds Ltd, 1977
Other material copyright © Anthony du Gard Pasley, 1977
First published in 1977

Allen Lane
Penguin Books Ltd
17 Grosvenor Gardens
London sw1w obd

ISBN 0 7139 1006 2
Printed photolitho in Great Britain by
Ebenezer Baylis & Son Ltd, The Trinity Press,
Worcester, and London

Contents

Acknowledgements

The illustrations in this book were done by the following artists: Norman Barber – Pansy, Nasturtium Dwarf, Nasturtium Gleam; Henry Barnett – Californian Poppy, Chrysanthemum, Larkspur, Linaria; David Baxter – Nemesia Carnival, Nasturtium Giant Climbing, Sweet Scabious, Sweet Sultan, Antirrhinum, Alyssum Saxatile; Leonora Box – Sunflower; Patricia Caley – Clarkia, Mesembryanthemum, Statice, Mignonette; David Cook – Aster Single, Aster Ostrich Plume, Alyssum Snow Carpet; Patrick Cox – Wallflower, Hollyhock, Delphinium, Calendula; Pauline Ellison – Sweet William, Polyanthus, Dahlia, Verbena; Leslie Greenwood – Aquilegia, Canary Creeper, Morning Glory, Shirly Poppy, Iceland Poppy, Lupin, Zinnia; Vera Ibbett – Canterbury Bells, Cornflower, Schizanthus, Foxglove, Phlox, Pyrethrum, Godetia; Ron Kirby – Viscaria, Phacelia Campanularia; Kristin Rosenberg – Helichrysum, Gypsophila, Viola; Faith Shannon – Cosmos, Nigella, Sweet Pea; Kathleen Smith – Candytuft, Lobelia String of Pearls, Lobelia Pendula Sapphire, Virginian Stock, Night Scented Stock, Forget-Me-Not, Nicotiana, Ten Week Stock, Daisy; Gill Smyth – Aubrietia; George Thompson – Petunia, Dianthus Baby Doll, Nemophila. Instructions for planting by D. B. Clay-Jones; text editors Terence Griffin and Francesca Zeissl.

Growing Plants from Seed

Why grow plants from seed?

This collection of flowers covers a long season from the Wallflowers of late spring to the Asters of late Autumn. They are nearly all familiar flowers – some like the Marigold and Foxglove have been grown for centuries, others such as Nemesia and Schizanthus are relatively new. The collection includes annuals which generally last one year only; biennials which are sown one year to bloom the next; and perennials which will give pleasure for many many years (see pp. 97–103 for a table). In this short introduction to growing and using flowering plants I shall be drawing in particular on the plants illustrated in the book, but I will mention others, the range of flowering plants being so wide.

Not so long ago plants were one of the cheapest pleasures of life. It was simple to buy a dozen of this or fifty of that and hardly worth the trouble to grow them from seed. However, this is no longer the case – growing plants from seed has become an economic necessity. It can also be a great source of pleasure. There is something very exciting about the thought that with a small handful of seeds you can create a border, a shrubbery – even a forest!

Growing plants from seed also allows a great deal of experiment. Many plants can be increased by means of division, but by far the quickest and best results are obtained from seeds, and instead of having a thin scattering of plants you can have a rich abundance. Moreover, plants which have adapted themselves to a particular climate and soil from seedling stage onwards are far more likely to do well than ones which may have travelled from a long distance. Though it is sensible to concentrate on plants which are most suited to your gardens, the urge to experiment – to try the doubtfully hardy plant, the unknown exotic – is much greater when there is only a packet of seed at stake. You can grow a great many seedlings and try them out in different parts of the garden.

Plants are curious things – sometimes they will mope in the most favourable place and grow like wildfire where they are not supposed to. Sometimes it is worth trying a pinch or two of seed where normal methods of planting are impossible – cracks in paving, crevices in old walls, narrow ledges in a rock garden, undisturbed verges of gravel paths. However, though plants do grow naturally in these odd positions they are never entirely deprived of food and water. A seedling may grow in an ancient wall where the mortar is old and rotten and the top of the wall cracked so that rain enters, and the seedling finds the damp sandy material of the joints easy to root into and nourishing enough for modest growth. A seed pushed into a small crevice in a modern wall may not take at all. Make sure therefore that however improbable the position the seed has a little finely sifted sand and soil to give it a start and the possibility of water until it has become well established when its roots will grow a long way in search of nourishment.

Although plants usually come true from seed, there is always the possibility that one will turn out to be entirely different – this has been the source of many new varieties. For that reason I am always reluctant to throw away any seedlings until they have proved themselves. Sometimes the least satisfactory turn out in the end to be the most interesting. Naturally once a plant has developed and shown itself to be inferior it should be thrown away.

Germination

All seeds require certain basic conditions in order to germinate. These are as follows.

One, air. This does not mean that the soil should have large air pockets – simply that the soil particles should be something like the size of granulated sugar with tiny air spaces in between. This allows the young rootlets to penetrate the soil and find the food they need. Soil which is hard and compact, such as heavy clay, can sometimes prevent germination altogether.

Two, moisture. Seeds will not germinate in completely dry surroundings. This usually presents no problems, though it can be troublesome with lawns or perennials sown in dry summer months.

Three, warmth – probably the most important condition and the one least well understood by amateurs. Plants grown from seed can be roughly divided into two groups: those which can be sown directly outside in the garden and those which require the warmth of a greenhouse or something similar before they will grow. When sowing outside, the soil temperature must be sufficiently high to sustain germination – every kind of seed has its own minimum below which it will not germinate at all. Unless this minimum is reached the seed will sit there and slowly rot. Plants which require extra warmth can either be sown in a greenhouse or on a warm, sunny sill or even in an airing cupboard (most seeds do not need light to germinate). Generally speaking these 'half hardy' plants (see below) require a temperature of about 50–55°F in order to germinate successfully. This temperature must be maintained night and day – if it drops at night to, say, 35–40°F, germinating seeds may not survive. Some half hardy plants require an even higher germinating temperature, up to 65–70°F: for example, Begonias, African Violets and Salvias. Their seed packets will usually tell you what they need.

Four, depth. There is no point in sowing seeds very deeply because the deeper you sow, the colder the soil – and the less chance the seeds have of germinating successfully. Moreover, the deeper you sow, the further the seedling has to grow before it reaches the soil surface to open its first pair of leaves and become self-supporting. Until it does so, it is entirely dependent on the food stored in the seed, so that if it runs out of food before it reaches the surface it will die. I would suggest, as a general guide, that seeds should be covered by a layer of soil equal to their own diameter, making sure that there is enough soil on top to keep them from being displaced by rain or wind.

Annuals, biennials and perennials

Different plants have different life cycles, making them suitable for different parts of the garden. These can be broadly classified into three groups.

Annuals complete their life cycle in one growing season: they grow from seed, flower, set seed and die. The seed set this year germinates and produces plants next year. Annuals are split into two groups: hardy annuals, which are native to our own country or countries with a similar climate, which means that they can be sown in the open garden in spring and early summer; and half hardy annuals, which are natives of a warmer climate and which therefore, in order to achieve a full season of growth and flowering, must be started in the warmth, usually in late February through March and early April.

The next group are the *hardy biennials*, plants such as Wallflowers, Sweet William, Canterbury Bells, Forget-Me-Nots. These seeds are sown in spring and early summer of one year, the plant grows through that year and then blooms in the spring or summer of the following year. It then dies, having seeded.

The third and last group are the *hardy perennials*. These grow and flower during the spring and summer; in autumn all growth above soil level dies down to disappear completely in the winter and reappear again in the spring. In other words, they overwinter as subterranean clumps, but are permanent residents of our borders. They need not be disturbed except to be rejuvenated by splitting and replanting as the centre of the clump gets old and worked out.

There is one more group of plants: those which come from tropical countries and are not really suitable for outdoor growing. They may be annuals or perennials but they spend their lives as pot plants, being grown either in the greenhouse or the house. This group includes plants like African Violets and the Regal Pelargoniums.

F1 Hybrids

These are first generation plants derived from crossing two parent plants, each of which has certain desirable characteristics. F1 hybrid seed is always more expensive than ordinary seed because the cross has to be made from the original parents every year. Seeds from the first F1 generation will not breed true, but only give 50 per cent of the required plants. Is it worth paying two or three times more for F1 hybrids? The answer is, I think, yes, because F1 hybrids have inherent hybrid vigour, which means that if you are growing vegetables you get better and more consistent crops, and if you are growing flowers you get improved plants with better flowers and colours. The hybrid vigour also means that they are less susceptible to pests and diseases and grow healthier and stronger.

Pelleted seed

A pelleted seed is one which has been enclosed in an inert casing material, the aim being simply to increase its size so that the seeds can be handled individually, and sown spaced out at whatever intervals you want in the seed tray and left to grow there until they are ready for planting out. They don't need pricking out – the gardening term for transplanting small seedlings growing thickly – and thus there is no growth check, as with normal transplanting. For seeds sown outdoors, for example hardy annuals and hardy vegetables, you can sow the pellets at the correct distances apart in rows so that you don't have to go through the process of thinning later on. This means less work and also no root disturbance either to the seedling moved or to those left behind.

Growing seeds outside

In natural conditions only about 10 per cent of seeds which fall to the ground germinate, so if you are hoping for high germination of your garden seeds you must prepare the ground carefully to make sure of the best possible start. There are two main locations for seed sowing outside. One, where the plants are to remain. This is best for hardy

annuals and vegetable seeds. Two, in a seed bed from which the seedlings
are transplanted to a spare bed or their permanent home.

Although it may seem simplest to sow plants directly into their final
position (and it is essential for hardy annuals), the preparation of irregular
patches of ground, often between existing groups of plants, presents
many problems. Firstly, the soil may be poor. If so, fork it over, break
down any lumps and put on a little fine bonemeal or a good pre-seeding
fertilizer, following the maker's instructions. Then lightly firm the
soil and rake it down ready to receive the seeds. Secondly, adjoining
plants may rob the young seedlings of light and air – a space which is
large and open in spring may become completely covered by mid
summer. If this is the case, the area should not be used for seed sowing
unless surrounding growth can be severely curtailed or carefully
supported early in the season. Slugs, snails and other pests, who love
young seedlings, may also lurk in the surrounding plants and are less easy
to control than in the open rows of a seed bed. In spite of these difficulties
annuals sown where they are to bloom can fill gaps in a new herbaceous
border or between shrubs, and an annual border makes a valuable
contribution in gardens of all sizes.

If possible, a special area for seed sowing and planting out should
be set aside for perennials and biennials which are not be sown directly
in position. Such a seed bed may well adjoin, or even form part of, a
kitchen garden, if you have one, since the requirements and methods of
cultivation are similar. A cropping plan may also allow interplanting
flower seeds for transplanted seedlings between vegetable rows.

It is unwise to sow seeds on loose, freshly dug ground. The soil
should be lightly firmed by treading down before it is raked over to
produce a fine tilth. Remove all large stones and other unwanted material.

As we've already seen (pages 2–3), all seeds, whether sown inside
or out, need air, moisture, warmth and correct depth in order to germinate satisfactorily. In general the depth at which they should be grown
is governed by their size, since they should be covered by a layer of
compost or soil equal to their own diameter. Fine, dust-like seeds need

only be covered with enough compost or soil to prevent them from being blown away or otherwise disturbed.

The other essential is thin sowing. Thickly sown seeds result in overcrowding with seedlings struggling for light and air. They also have to be thinned and possibly transplanted. Seeds sown thinly enough will form strong little plants some of which can remain in place while the intermediate ones will be sturdy enough to transplant and grown on without shock.

The time for sowing will depend on the type of plant and also the weather: in general the air temperature must be consistently high enough to warm the soil, since sowing in cold soil inhibits or even stops growth. This will obviously vary from year to year. The best advice I can give is a tip handed down to me by an old gardener who said: never sow outside until you see the weed seeds beginning to germinate – and sure enough, it works.

When you sow seeds where the plants are to remain it is essential to obtain an even coverage of the area. Gardeners are sometimes advised to make a thin random scattering of seed. However carefully this is done, it always produces patchy results. It is much better to treat the space, however irregular, as though it were a seed bed, setting the rows of seeds as wide apart as the final spacing of the plants. Although the seedlings will have to be thinned out along the length of the rows, the side spacing will be correct. If pelleted seed is available, the seeds can also be set at the correct spacing in the rows.

Sowing in a seed bed is always done in drills – basically for ease of working, as random sowing makes too many problems at the thinning stage. Using a measuring rod or tape, put pegs in along both sides of the bed at the right distance apart for the rows. Stretch a garden line between the pegs and draw a shallow drill along one side of it to the correct depth. Any pointed stick can be used or a swan-necked hoe. You can also use an ordinary wooden label – edge on for shallow drills and broadside for deeper drills and larger seeds. If seeds are large and rounded make a flat drill with a spade to prevent them rolling.

If the ground is dry, give it a thorough soaking the day before preparing the drills. You can warm the soil if necessary by placing cloches over it for seven to fourteen days before sowing. Except on very light soils it is not wise to water the bed just before sowing.

Once again, thin sowing is essential for good results, and there is no need to use all the seed in a packet at one sowing. After sowing, cover the drills carefully, using the back of a rake to ensure even cover, then gently firm along the line of the drill and finally very lightly rake in the same direction as the drill, to avoid disturbing the seed. If you are doing a lot of sowing, put labels at the ends of the rows before you begin giving the name and variety of the plant, date of sowing and other relevant details. Don't try to save trouble by spiking the seed packet with a piece of twig and leaving this as a label. The packets are sure to disintegrate and blow away, leaving you wondering what you planted.

Most plants grown in the seedbed will be biennials or perennials for use in bedding schemes or as permanent plants. These will have to be transplanted as seedlings to a spare piece of ground in order to grow on to flowering size before planting out in their final positions. If the sowing was thin enough you will be able to move intermediate plants, leaving the remainder to grow on where they were sown. If the seedlings are rather crowded any movement may disturb the roots of the remainder, in which case it is best to dig up the whole row, a short section at a time, and plant out all the young seedlings in a fresh piece of ground. Young seedlings must be handled carefully, held by the soil round the roots rather than the stem which can easily be bruised or broken, and never left with roots exposed to the air for more than a few moments. Never transplant when the air is cold or there is a drying wind; always plant into damp soil and water the plants late in the day when there is no sun on them.

Growing seeds under glass

If you have some glass available – even a small unheated greenhouse or cold frame – the season for sowing and the range of plants you can grow will be considerably extended. Any glass structure which is specifically intended for raising plants from seed should be sited near your potting shed or working area where the pots are washed and compost, seeds and other essentials stored. There are neat ready-made structures consisting of a shed at one end and a greenhouse at the other. If you have some broad window ledges and the temperature in the room remains fairly constant, you can use these instead of outside glass. Protect the ledge from damage and stand the pots on a layer of fine gravel in a plastic plant tray. Because the air in the house is dry, the gravel must be kept moist or the tender seedlings will shrivel. Seeds can also be germinated in an airing cupboard.

All seed sowing under glass is done in pots or seed trays, either on the staging of a greenhouse or in a garden frame. Whatever you use, it should be clean. Any container to be reused should be washed out thoroughly with water. Good drainage is also important. Put a one-inch layer of old crocks or small stones in the bottom of the pot or tray.

Seed sowing takes place in seed compost specially formulated from a mixture of sand, peat and fibrous loam to give the best rooting medium, and containing a balanced fertilizer suitable for young seedlings – usually the John Innes composts. Sieved garden soil, wherever it comes from, is bound to contain weed seeds which will germinate along with the seeds you have sown making it difficult if not impossible to distinguish the plant seedlings from those of the weeds. All the materials in seed compost have been sterilized so that there are no weed seeds, pests or diseases. You can also use soil-less composts which are peat-based (again sterile) and contain a balanced fertilizer. These have certain advantages over the John Innes composts – they warm up faster allowing faster germination and their texture is such that you get a better root system on the seedlings.

Fill the containers with moist compost to within half an inch of the rim and pat down with a piece of board or other flat object to get a level surface. Then place the containers in an old sink or bowl and fill the sink

or bowl with water to just below the level of the soil inside the containers.
Leave until the water has risen from below and moistened the surface of the compost. Lift out and allow to drain. The containers can also be watered from above using a can with a fine rose, but this tends to compact the surface of the soil and does not soak the compost evenly.

The general principles for sowing the seed are the same as for outside, except that instead of being planted in rows the seeds are scattered thinly over the surface of the damp compost and then just covered to the correct depth with finely sifted compost or, in the case of very small seeds, a scattering of silver sand. Flat seeds, like those of Lilies and Cucumbers, should be pressed gently on one side with a pencil so that they stand up on one edge. They germinate much better this way than if left lying flat on the compost.

After sowing, lightly firm the compost and cover the container with a sheet of brown paper and then a sheet of glass (neither touching the compost). In this way moisture is retained in the compost and atmosphere surrounding the seeds, and light is excluded—the best conditions for germination. Keep a careful watch and as soon as the seedlings have begun to show remove the glass and paper to prevent the seedlings from becoming drawn up and spindly. If they do so, either from being left too long or sown too thickly, they may fall prey to 'damping off', a disease caused by a fungus which spreads rapidly attacking the stems and causing the seedlings to collapse and rot. This can be prevented by watering with Cheshunt Compound. Once the seedlings are visible, place the containers near the glass but do not expose them to draughts or very strong sunshine.

As soon as the seedlings are large enough to handle (plants under glass grow faster than in the open), transplant them. This first transplanting should be done very carefully as young seedlings can easily be damaged by rough handling. Prepare containers in the same way as for seed sowing, making sure that the potting compost is already damp before pricking out. A small pointed stick or pencil can be used to make evenly spaced holes two inches apart and of the right depth in the compost.

The seedlings themselves can be lifted with the help of a wooden label with a v-shaped notch cut in the end so that it becomes a simple two-pronged fork. This notch will allow the seedling to be eased into the hole and held upright while the other hand firms the compost gently round the roots without touching the plant. After transplanting, the seedlings will need a little extra shading for a day or two until they have recovered from the move. They can then be grown on under the same conditions, the temperature being gradually lowered and the amount of air increased until they are ready to withstand outside conditions. Seedlings of tender indoor and greenhouse plants must be grown on in the temperature and conditions appropriate to their kind. Most seedlings can remain in their boxes until the leaves touch, at which point they should either be potted up singly or transplanted into their final positions outside. If they are left, the young plants will quickly become drawn up and spindly and never regain their lost vigour.

All half hardy plants, whether flowers or vegetables, will need 'hardening off' before planting in the open. This means giving them a period of acclimatization somewhere between the greenhouse and the open garden to accustom them to the difference of temperature. There are three ways of doing this. The first is to put the containers in a garden frame, the top of which is left off on warm sunny days, just opened six to twelve inches on cloudy blustery days, and shut down at night. Secondly, the seed boxes or trays can be put in a straight row on the ground and covered with cloches. Thirdly, if you haven't got a frame or cloches, take the boxes out of the warmth during the day, place them in a warm sheltered part of the garden and then take them back into the greenhouse at night. The normal period for hardening off is ten to fourteen days.

Using Flowering Plants

The ease with which plants can be grown from seed opens up a whole range of possibilities for their use, but it is essential to decide first of all what type of plants you need.

Perennials are generally sown in late spring or summer and often do not produce good flowers for the first season, but after that they grow into large clumps and give abundant blooms for many years. Most of the familiar plants from the herbaceous border, for example Aquilegia, Delphinium, Hollyhock and Lupin, belong to this class. Biennials are sown in the spring of one year to flower in the following spring or summer and are frequently used in bedding out schemes. This system of planting, in which beds or containers are replanted two or three times a year to maintain a more or less continuous display, is not labour-saving but it can be useful in key positions near the house. Polyanthus, Sweet William and Wallflower are typical biennials. Hardy annuals are for quick effects. Sown in the spring, often where they are to bloom, they flower within a few weeks and continue until the first frosts. Many childhood favourites such as Candytuft and Cornflower, Nasturtium and Shirley Poppy belong to this class. Annuals are invaluable where there are blank spaces to fill at minimum cost. Success always depends on choosing the right type of plant for your particular purpose: tables of the perennials, biennials and annuals illustrated in this book are given on pp. 98–103.

Seclusion

In a new garden, or where extensive alterations are in progress, there is often a need to give some seclusion and a feeling of maturity to an otherwise barren plot. Providing that the ground is well prepared this is perfectly possible. All the areas in which plants are to be grown must be dug over, preferably in the autumn before planting. The ground can then be left rough so that frost can penetrate the soil, breaking down the clods and killing off pests. In the spring, as soon as it is dry enough to work, fork through the soil again, removing all weeds, old roots and builders' rubbish. Then lightly consolidate the ground – the pressure of your feet as you walk about preparing the soil may be enough – and rake it down. If any well-rotted compost or really old manure is available, sift it finely and add it to the surface of the soil. You will probably have to rely on peat, some sharp sand if your soil is heavy, bonfire and wood ash, and bonemeal, applied at the rate of $1\frac{1}{2}$ oz. to the square yard. All these should be raked into the surface soil. If you have reason to think that the soil is very acid – and you do not propose to grow lime-hating plants in the same part of the garden – you can give a light surface dressing of lime, leaving it to be washed into the soil by the rain.

Runner Beans, either grown up strings attached to the boundary fence, on bamboo canes held together by light battens top and bottom, or on nets secured to a long pole held by a tripod of poles at either end, will form a quick screen. A thinner screen can be made using Sweet Peas, trailing Nasturtiums or Canary Creeper, to name but a few possibilities. An ugly shed can be clothed by Cobea Scandens, a half hardy climber which needs to be started under glass or on a warm window-ledge in the house. Given reasonable support and a sunny position, this amazing plant will cover an area at least ten feet square before being killed off by the frost.

Height

An impression of height can be achieved by growing patches of the old-fashioned Sunflower which, given reasonable soil, will shoot up to at least eight feet in a season, or the very lovely Lavatera. Hollyhocks will also reach about six feet, as will some varieties of Sweet Corn; and tripods of tall canes or bean poles thickly planted round with Sweet Peas or Morning Glory can make an effective vertical feature.

A number of annuals will grow sufficiently large and bushy where something fairly massive is required: plants of Cosmos, set far enough apart to grow their full four feet and show their strong branch structure and feathery foliage to advantage; Lavatera, which looks rather like a small Hibiscus; Nicotiana sylvestris, a large tobacco plant with some of the character but none of the dangers of that handsome greenhouse shrub Datura; the big double flowered Opium Poppies, with their handsome silver-blue leaves; Foxgloves; the tall Larkspurs, and many others.

If you can wait a year, there are several fast-growing shrubs which come easily from seed and will generally reach a reasonable size and flower in their second year: the many coloured Brooms, and the 'Spanish Broom', which is in fact a Spartium and flowers in July and August when the others are over, the fairly tender Tree Lupin, which grows very large very quickly and is covered with white or pale yellow or mauve flowers, and the new hybrid Hibiscus, which will continue to grow and produce its enormous red and pink flowers for years if given a warm, dry place.

Annual Borders

Annual borders have been a favourite feature of many public parks and gardens for years. The main trouble with borders of this kind is that, however bright, they have a thin and insubstantial look which gives away their temporary nature. Fortunately there are some good foliage plants which will add weight and solidity to the border. Given some glass or sufficient broad window ledges, you can grow Eucalyptus, Cineraria maritima, Centaurea and the huge silver thistle Onopordon Arabicum for grey foliage; Atriplex rubra and Perilla atropurpurea for red-purple; the castor oil plant Ricinus Gibsoni, Grevillea robusta, the Jacaranda, Kochia, the summer cypress, and many others for green. Some of these are, in fact, tender shrubs or trees which can be potted up and overwintered in the house for use another year, although several will survive a mild winter if given a sheltered position out of doors. If used in bold groups or long diagonal drifts they will introduce a feeling of permanence to counterbalance the transient patterns of flower colour.

Unless you have room for two annual borders – one for early and the other for late summer – you will want your border to be as bright as possible right through the season. There are various ways of achieving this. Firstly, you can choose species which have the longest possible flowering season and cut off the dead flowers regularly – daily if possible – so that the plants are unable to set seed and therefore continue flowering. Secondly, you can make two or three sowings of a quick-growing hardy annual like Clarkia or Californian Poppy, to extend the flowering season. You will have to leave space for these later sowings, either by planting only a part of the patch where you intend them to bloom to begin with, or by providing space in other parts of the border, or by removing early flowerers the moment they begin to fade, freshening the soil and sowing again. Thirdly, you can hide spaces where plants are fading by ensuring that rather slower growing and later blooming plants are sown beside and in front of them. Fourthly – if you have time and space available – you can keep a supply of pots planted with annuals or biennials and tuck these into any bare spaces in your border just as they are coming into flower: Canterbury Bells, Asters and Zinnias are particularly effective used in this way. Calendula, annual Chrysanthemum, Clarkia, Godetia (both tall and dwarf), Cornflowers and Nigella, Scabious and Sweet Sultan are all ideal subjects for a border of this kind. You can of course include groups of biennials which were sown the previous year, and half hardy annuals sown under glass and planted out as soon as the danger of frost is past; but the simple border of hardy annuals is the easiest to manage.

Perennial Borders

A perennial border is a longer-term project, because the seeds must first be sown in a spare piece of ground, and then the young plants grown on for a year or even two years before being put into their final

positions in the border. Not all herbaceous plants come easily from
seed and some, like Paeonies, take several years to bloom; but most of the
familiar border flowers are quite easy. Aquilegias, Delphiniums,
Gypsophila paniculata, Russell Lupins and Pyrethrum can all be relied
upon to give some bloom the year after they are sown. While you are
waiting for your perennial plants to grow, you can fill the temporary gaps
with annuals or with bold groups of biennials. Pansies, Ten Week Stocks,
Sweet William and Wallflower are very effective when used in this way
and will often flower again the following year if you have cut off the
dead flowers regularly.

Colour Schemes
Many of the pictures in this book illustrate flowers in mixed colours, so
you can see the number of colours which are obtainable separately under
such names as Wallflowers 'Rose Queen' or 'Primrose Dame'. The
most successful mixtures are those based on a single colour. For instance
mixed varieties of Calendula – the old-fashioned Pot Marigold of cottage
gardens – are agreeable because the range is restricted to the bronze–
orange–yellow grouping. Mixed Wallflowers, on the other hand, can
contain almost any colour except blue, and they tend to look a muddle
because each plant takes away from rather than builds up to the colour
of the one next to it. On the whole it is much wiser to decide on a
definite scheme for your border and then choose single colours which
will fit in with it.

What the scheme is to be entirely depends, of course, on the surroundings. The most important thing is that there should be a scheme, and
that you stick to it. The pretty but unrelated plant – 'I simply must have
one of those' – is the downfall of many garden schemes and the reason
why so much hard work often produces so little visual result. If you are
uncertain about how to mix or blend colours, why not simply use one
colour at a time, but use it in every available shade and tone? An all-red
border, for instance, ranging from pale orange-red to deep crimson,
would be very striking, particularly if you used red and purple foliage

plants as an accompaniment. Scarlet and crimson Dahlias and Begonias, some of which have dark bronze leaves; Antirrhinums Scarlet Monarch and Crimson Monarch; Atriplex hortensis rubra, the mountain spinach with rich red leaves; Amaranthus caudatus, Love-Lies-Bleeding of cottage gardens; Verbena Blaze; Nasturtium Empress of India and Nicotiana crimson bedder are a few of the plants which would look well in such a scheme. All yellow – pale cream to pale orange – is sunny and attractive, with abundant use of the silver foliage of Verbascum Silver Spire, Centaurea candidissima and Cineraria maritima for contrast. Alyssum Saxatile might form a permanent edging to drifts of Antirrhinums Golden Monarch and Pale Sulphur, with Bartonia aurea; Calendula Lemon Queen; Pansy Coronation Gold; Petunia Brass Band and Nasturtium Golden Gleam. The season could be extended into spring with groups of Wallflowers Cloth of Gold, Primrose Monarch and Ivory White, yellow Polyanthus and yellow Violas.

Both these ranges can be extended for greater variety. A red scheme could include purple, violet, and – for a spicy clash – the occasional touch of magenta, such as Verbena Mme du Barry. A yellow border could be varied with orange and some of those bronze and reddish browns which are frequently found in annual Chrysanthemums, Nasturtiums and Helichrysums. Alternatively, you can choose a range of related colours – mauves, pinks, purples, blues and grey, for instance – and then play up and down the tonal scale, contrasting light with dark or working up to the deepest tones in the middle and out to the palest at the ends of the border.

Arrangement

You must also decide on the general outlines of your border – not its shape on the ground, for that is already dug and prepared, but the relationships of the height and shape of the plants within it. The old idea was to grow all the tall plants at the back (or in the centre if the bed was double-sided) and then work downwards to the lowest at the edge, producing a slope that looks like a coloured railway embankment. This

Figure 1 Elevation of border showing variation in height of plant material giving a varied outline.

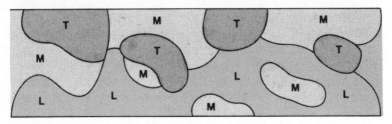

Figure 2 Plan of border showing placing of tall, medium and low plants to emphasize form and texture of plants. Many different types and varieties of plants in the three heights would be used.

can be very dull, and it does not show the shape of the individual plants to advantage, since all form and foliage are lost in the general slope.

You should aim to set plants of varying heights together, so that in silhouette they look rather like a graph, high peaks contrasted with adjoining low points. On the ground you should also vary the placing, with groups of tall plants coming quite close to the front of the border in some places and lower ones sweeping round and between them as though they were the waters of a stream flowing round and between projecting rocks. The form of the larger plants is seen to advantage in this way, and the whole border is given much greater character than in the embankment method.

If the annuals are used only as infill, or as groundcover to shrub borders, the same method should be followed, with the permanent plants playing the dominant role. Consider their form and shape first and then choose the varieties of temporary plants to complement them in colour and habit of growth. Suppose, for instance, that you have a bare space left in the border where a patch of bulbs has been allowed to die down naturally, and that the adjoining plants are Iris Germanica. You could sow trailing Nasturtiums of a suitable colour outside the patch while the bulb foliage is still green, and then draw the long trails of the Nasturtiums across the bare space as they develop. Alternatively you could wait until the bulb foliage has died right down, then freshen up the soil with a hand fork and sow a quick-growing annual such as Linaria to cover the ground and provide late summer flowers. In the first case the circular blue-green leaves of the Nasturtiums would make a perfect complement to the grey-green sword leaves of the Iris; in the second example the fine growth of Linaria would throw the strong upright pattern of the Iris into high relief.

Where, as sometimes happens, an existing bed contains a scattering of permanent plants that are quite unrelated to one another, an effect of unity can be given by covering the whole bed – or even a series of beds – with a single annual. Lobelia Cambridge Blue and the white or pale mauve Alyssum are particularly useful for this purpose; their colour, while insistent enough to give an impression of harmony, is not so strong as to compete with the varied colours of the flowers around them. Rose beds in which (as too often happens) the roses are of ill-assorted colours are much improved by this method of under-planting, for which blue or white Violas are an ideal choice.

Bedding Out

During the nineteenth century most gardens contained a large number of flower beds filled with bright patterns of bulbs and half hardy annuals, changed two or three times a year to maintain a continuous display. Although this system – known as 'bedding out' – has long been out of fashion except in public parks, there is much to be said for its use on a small scale. In no other way can one achieve such a concentration of colour and variety of effect in a limited area: given the time and enthusiasm, you can have at least three different schemes in the course of a year, and the variations for each season are almost limitless. However, in order to keep even a modest area well furnished you will need a large space for seed beds, planting-out ground and greenhouse or frames, so it is wise not to be too ambitious. A few beds on a terrace or some tubs and urns in a paved garden will probably be sufficient to give you ample scope, since nothing looks worse than bedding out done in a half-hearted manner.

Good Bedding Plants

Before deciding on any particular scheme for bedding out, it is as well to consider the attributes of a good bedding plant, since not all annuals or biennials are equally suitable. Firstly, the plant should have a neat habit of growth (unless you propose to cover the whole space with a single plant, in which case a sprawling form may be quite convenient). Secondly, it should flower continuously through the period for which the bedding is designed, with blooms which are fairly evenly spaced over the plant and drop off when they have faded rather than remain to give an untidy look to the bed. Thirdly, if you live in an unpredictable climate it is best to avoid plants which are particularly sensitive to the weather. Pansies, Violas and other plants which enjoy a cool damp summer look wretched in a hot season; Zinnias make a poor show if it is cold and damp; and many sun-loving plants such as Gazanias and Mesembryanthemums refuse to open their flowers at all on dull days. Fourthly, you should not mix plants needing different conditions. Fuchsias and Begonias want light shade and a moist soil, while the popular grey- and silver-leafed plants need a well-drained and sunny position, otherwise they tend to turn green and even rot off.

All these may seem perfectly simple and obvious requirements, but it is surprising how many apparently suitable plants fail in one respect or another. As with other forms of gardening it is essential to learn to observe plants and to note all their attributes. It is not sufficient to know their general requirements for growth and to have a vague idea about their flowering habits. You must know the colour and texture of the leaves and whether the plant remains well furnished at all times or if, by losing the lower leaves, it gets thin at the bottom and needs under-planting. You should note the colour, shape and texture of the buds, the length of time the flower remains open, the effect of sun which may bleach or rain which may spoil the open flower, the retention or other-wise of dead flowers, the appearance of seed pods or fruits, and the length of time during which under normal circumstances the plant can be expected to look its best. Observation is one of the attributes of a good gardener. Even your daily walk to the station or bus stop can teach you much about the habits of the plants in the gardens you pass on the way.

This does not mean that you should use only old and well-known favourites, but it does suggest that any plant you intend to use as part of a bedding scheme should be tried out first in some less conspicuous place, since a failure in a bedding scheme can be a disaster for the whole season. However, gaps caused by bad weather or some other mis-fortune can often be filled without too much trouble, given a little foresight. One frequently grows more seedlings than there are spaces to fill, and if you can spare a little extra time to pot up some of this surplus, either one or three strong seedlings to a pot depending on the species of plant, and then line out the pots in a spare corner of the seed bed where they can be watered and fertilized as necessary, you will have a good reserve of plants. Then if failures occur or there are gaps in the border or bedding scheme you can sink a spare plant, complete with pot, into the soil at any moment, even when it is in full bloom. Any plants not needed for repair work can be grouped to give additional colour beside terrace doorways or at the sides of garden steps, or they can simply go to swell the stock of the produce stall at a local fête.

The usual pattern of bedding is either to create a coloured mound in which plants of varying heights rise by stages from the lowest at the edge to a central ridge or peak, depending on the shape of the bed, or to have a more or less flat carpet – sometimes with a border of a different plant, though generally of the same height – in which stand much higher specimens of a contrasting form and colour. For instance, a rich crimson–pink scheme for summer might have a border of crimson Lobelia, then a band of Verbena Mme du Barry, followed by Petunia Rose Perfection and Antirrhinum Leonard Sutton, with Lavatera Loveliness in the centre of the mound. Alternatively a bed of the dwarf Antirrhinum Rose might be edged with Dianthus Baby Doll and have 'dot' plants of Schizanthus. Sometimes the low carpet can be pierced by evenly spaced plants of another kind – for example, in spring, beds of Wallflowers or Forget-Me-Nots may form a base for a display of Tulips or Hyacinths – while with careful selection a three-tiered effect of decreasing density can be achieved.

With the right plants and proper attention to form and colour, any of these methods can produce striking and effective results, but all are extremely formal and demand an equally formal setting if they are not to look out of place. Another way is to use the same plants in an informal and apparently casual way, replacing symmetry with asymmetry and formality with balance. Such a system can even be carried out within a formal pattern of flower beds, and tends to be much more in harmony with the setting of modern gardens. The difference between the two systems is shown in Figures 3 and 4.

Form and texture

One must remember that all plants have form and texture as well as colour. The strong, spire-like shapes of Hollyhocks, Foxgloves and Verbascum are obvious examples of the dominance of form, but the sculptured leaves of Sunflower and Paeony-flowered Poppy, the horizontal carpet of Candytuft, rounded cushions of Aubrietia and larger

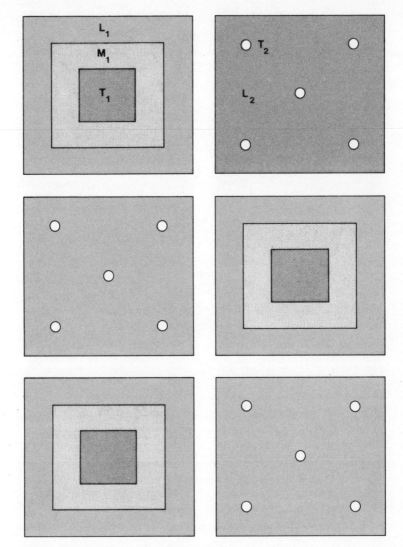

Figure 3 Formal bedding scheme. Squares of low carpet with dot plants alternate with pyramid arrangements of low, medium and tall. The plants in the corresponding three squares would all be the same varieties.

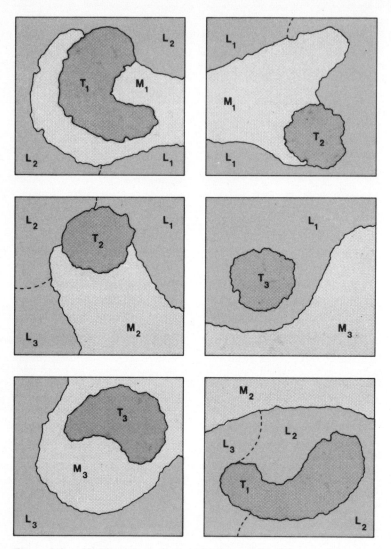

Figure 4 Informal bedding scheme. Asymmetric placing of three different varieties of low, medium and tall plants in the same three beds.

rounded clouds of Gypsophila are all examples of other easily recognized forms. Texture comes not only from the physical feel of particular leaves – furry Stachys lanata, granular Mesembryanthemum, felt-like Cineraria maritima – but also from the general effect of the plant when viewed from a distance. Nasturtium has a coarse texture because the large round leaves present a sharp pattern of light and shade, while Californian Poppy, Nigella and Linaria are all fine. Sometimes it is not the foliage but the flowers which have a distinctive texture. The velvet tails of Love-Lies-Bleeding, the rather coarser papery flowers of annual Statice, the plush heads of Sweet Scabious and the glossy metallic petals of Helichrysum all have a strong character which their foliage lacks. In the old bedding systems, colour, whether of leaf or flower, was the dominant characteristic. Form was of importance only for isolated specimen plants, and texture remained a minor consideration. With an informal method the pattern is more subtle and relies on the inter-weaving and contrasting of all three attributes to gain maximum effect. Naturally one should not attempt to contrast all these elements at the same time, and often a grouping which relies on subtle changes of form and texture within a closely related colour scheme is the most satisfying.

With a silver theme, for instance, you might use Stachys lanata, which is low and furry; Verbascum Silver Spire, which has a striking form and is covered in silver–white wool; the Opium Poppy, with smoothly sculptured grey–blue leaves; Cineraria maritima, cut-leafed, matt-textured and silver–white; and Aquilegia, which repeats the colour of the Poppy leaves at a lower level with finer texture. Such a grouping emphasizes the importance of texture and form within a narrow range of foliage colour, while all the flowers are of quiet tones which will not distract from the silver effect. A similar red–bronze group could contain Ajuga reptans purpurea, an excellent groundcover plant with bronze leaves and grey–blue flowers which are a good foil to other colours; Lobelia cardinalis, with scarlet spires of bloom and metallic crimson leaves; Atriplex hortensis rubra, with taller spires of red foliage; the feathery bronze-leafed Fennel; Nasturtium Empress of India, with crimson flowers and dark leaves; and perhaps some Beetroot for its handsome purple–red leaves. Here colour, texture and form all work together.

When applying this method to a small pattern of formally shaped beds, the best plan is to give each bed a dominant plant, whether tall, medium or short; then contrast this with other related plants, always ensuring that the dominant plant from one bed is repeated in a minor key in the beds adjoining, as shown in Figure 4. In this way the informal pattern of the planting will flow across the formal pattern of the beds with a kind of swirling motion, giving a feeling of life and movement to what might otherwise tend to be rigid and lifeless. Indeed, it is just that rigidity, and the appearance of having been painted on the ground, which helped to bring the whole idea of bedding into disrepute.

Colour

Whether formal or informal, all bedding schemes need careful planning, and at least at first you may find it easiest to do this on squared paper so that you can decide how many plants of each variety you will need for each season. It is generally best to have a theme, and carry this right through the seasonal planting, rather than scatter a number of un-related patches of colour about the garden. This does not mean that your garden has to be dull – the themes can change from season to season and from year to year. With the great range of plants now available, you can decide on almost any colour scheme for any season; but in my own opinion it is wisest to work with, rather than against, nature.

In Britain the colours of spring are pale, the strongest note being the almost unbearably vivid colour of grass and unfolding leaves. Primroses, wild Daffodils, Windflowers, Bluebells (though these can seem quite bright in certain lights) and fruit blossom are all pale, clear colours. It is quite easy to devise a spring scheme in red and orange, but it is not nearly so spring-like as one which emphasizes the natural colouring. Primrose, pink or 'white' (really pale ivory) Wallflowers, white and yellow Polyanthus, blue or white Winter-flowering Pansies and Forget-Me-Nots can provide a basis for many attractive spring schemes.

The colours of summer are much stronger. Full-bodied rose pinks, reds and crimsons are particularly good in some varieties of Petunias, Godetia, annual Phlox and Verbena. Even the familiar bedding Geraniums – which are now so expensive to buy, but can be grown easily from seed sown under glass – provide many fine pink and crimson shades, as well as the normal scarlet. Blues from Lobelia, Nemophila and Cornflowers, deep purples of Canterbury Bells, Petunias and Heliotrope, can all be built up into rich harmonies. If these colours are too strong for your taste when used alone, they can be toned down with pale yellow Antirrhinums and Limnanthes, the pretty mauve Ageratum and silver foliage plants. There are so many plants available that the difficulty is to choose rather than to find enough.

Autumn is the time to unleash all the bonfire brilliance in a riot of scarlet, orange, gold and flame. Not everyone will want a separate autumn bedding scheme, of course, but if your summer scheme relied rather heavily on early-flowering plants – such as Ten Week Stocks or Nemesias – a late summer–autumn arrangement is well worth while. This is the time when annual Chrysanthemums, Sunflowers, Zinnias and Helichrysum come into their own, but by adjusting your times of sowing you can use most of the summer annuals and bedding plants in the appropriate range of colours. Antirrhinums, French and African Marigolds, Dahlias, Salvias, Pansies and the dwarf red Nicotiana can all be treated in this way. If your garden is in a cold area, however, do not include very half hardy subjects or those like Nasturtiums which collapse at the first frost.

When considering plant groupings, whether for bedding or the border, do not think only of flowers; certain herbs and vegetables can also be very attractive and useful at the same time. Obviously it would never do to use Lettuce, or anything which has to be gathered and used fairly quickly, as this would leave gaps in the planting (unless, of course, you had a reserve of pot plants, as already suggested). But plants like Carrots and Beetroot, both of which have very attractive foliage, do not have to be lifted until the end of summer, and are excellent for the purpose. Parsley has the most beautiful fresh green foliage and is particularly useful as a band at the edge of a formal bedding scheme, as is the golden-leafed Marjoram, which is a perennial and can be retained to make a richly coloured patch at the front of a herbaceous border. Chives, too, come easily from seed, and although generally grown for their onion-flavoured foliage they also have delightful mauvish-pink flowers.

It is not only low-growing plants which can be used in this way. The bronze-leafed Fennel, normally grown for use in fish dishes, is a most elegant plant which grows to about four feet and has attractive greenish-gold flowers; Angelica makes another handsome tall specimen plant with bold foliage. Do not, however, allow either of these to set seed unless you are prepared to be over-run with seedlings ever after. If you are patient, you can grow the superb Globe Artichoke from seed and enjoy its magnificent silver foliage and tall spikes of thistle heads – and enjoy eating the globes too!

Scent

Do not forget the pleasures of scent. Most people know the humble mauve Night Scented Stock which opens to release a ravishing smell in the evening. The seeds are best mixed with those of the Virginian Stock, which is about the same height and whose flowers remain open during the day, so that you do not have a patch of seemingly dead plants during daylight hours. The Tobacco Plant is well known for its fragrance, but if you want flowers as well it is wise to mix the seeds of Affinis, the strongly scented night-blooming white variety, with those of one of the coloured varieties which remain open during the day but have little scent. Other excellent plants for scent are Mignonette, which, like many fragrant flowers, is not particularly showy, Heliotrope Cherrypie and of course Sweet Peas, the most highly scented of which are the old-fashioned type with dull colours and rather small flowers. Ten Week

Stocks have a delicious spicy fragrance but unfortunately they are only in full bloom for about two months. However, by sowing some in February and March under glass and others in the open garden at the end of April, you can have a succession of flowers from late June. Brompton Stocks and Sweet Rocket, which are biennials, give a similar scent in the spring garden to mingle with the distinctive, rather heavier, scent of Wallflowers.

Many flowers not normally grown for scent have a particular fragrance of their own. This is seldom mentioned in the catalogues and it is often a matter of trial and error to find the scented varieties. The annual Alyssum has a strong smell of honey which extends some distance from the plant on warm days. Sweet Sultan lives up to its name, and so to a lesser degree does Sweet William, although the scent is spicy rather than sweet. A few varieties of Violas and Pansies, Petunias, Nasturtiums and Polyanthus are scented, and Marigolds certainly have a strong smell. Whether this can be described as scent is perhaps a matter of opinion!

Sixty-four Flowers

Alyssum
Gold Dust
Saxatile

9-12 ins.

Saxatile is very different from
the familiar Alyssum Snow Carpet.
It has bright yellow blooms every year
in early spring.

The plants are low (9-12 ins.) and compact,
and so look best in rockeries,
or banks and walls.

This variety looks good grown with Aubrietia
because of the attractively contrasting colours.

Alyssum Saxatiles like good fertile soil, and plenty of sun. They are hardy plants and will flower for years (Hardy Perennial).

Outdoors Sow thinly $\frac{1}{8}$ in. deep from April to August in a vacant part of the garden. When the seedlings are 1–2 ins. high, transplant them wherever you want them to flower next year.

Under glass Sow in boxes of good seed compost, somewhere warm, from Feb. to March. When there are four leaves, transplant the seedlings 2 ins. apart into boxes of potting compost. Once they grow big enough to fill the box, harden them off, either by putting the boxes in a frame, or keeping them in a sheltered part of the garden by day, taking them in at night in case of frost. Do this for a week or two, then plant them out wherever you want them to flower.

Alyssum
Snow Carpet

Alyssum has many tightly packed pure white flowers. The plants are bushy and compact with long and narrow leaves. They flower from June to Sept. and grow very close to the ground, only 3-4 ins. high, so look best in rock-gardens, on walls and in tubs and window boxes.

3-4 ins.

Alyssum is one of the most popular plants for edging beds and borders.

Alyssum likes ordinary well-drained soil and full sun. It is a hardy plant which you sow every year (Hardy Annual).

Outdoors Sow thinly $\frac{1}{8}$ in. deep in April or early May wherever you want them to flower. You can leave the plants un-thinned, or thin 3 ins. apart when they are big enough to handle easily.

Under glass If you want early flowers, sow in good seed compost, somewhere warm, from Feb. to March. When there are four leaves, transplant the seedlings 2 ins. apart into boxes of potting compost. To harden them off, put the boxes in a frame or keep them in a sheltered part of the garden by day, taking them in at night in case of frost. Do this for a week or two, then plant them out wherever you want them to flower.

Antirrhinum
Snapdragon
Intermediate Mixed

Antirrhinums have clusters of blooms encircling their flowering stems. Antirrhinums flower on and on, from June to October. They grow 15-18 ins.
This variety does well in tubs and window boxes as well as beds and borders.

15-18 ins.

There are very many colours of Antirrhinum, delicate and bright. Here are some of them.

Antirrhinums like rich, well-drained soil and sun or part shade. They are fairly hardy plants which you sow every year (Half Hardy Annual).
Outdoors Sow thinly ⅛ in. deep in April or early May wherever you want them to flower. You can leave the plants unthinned, or thin 9-10 ins. apart when they are big enough to handle easily.
Under glass If you want early flowers, sow in good seed compost, somewhere warm, from Feb. to March. When there are four leaves, transplant the seedlings 2 ins. apart into boxes of potting compost. To harden them off, put the boxes in a frame or keep them in a sheltered part of the garden by day, taking them in at night in case of frost. Do this for a week or two, then plant them out wherever you want them to flower.

When the flowers are over, cut the old stems away to let new ones grow.

Aquilegia
Columbine
Long Spurred Mixed

Aquilegias are very easy to grow and bring colour into your garden in May and June, well before summer plants.
Aquilegias have graceful, five petalled flowers with long spurs. The flowers are poised on slender stems above a mass of delicate leaves.

2–3 ft.

They are excellent for cutting.
Aquilegias have beautiful double coloured flowers like the ones shown.

Aquilegias need rich, well-drained soil and sun or part shade. They are hardy plants and will flower for years (Hardy Perennial).
Outdoors Sow thinly ⅛ in. deep from April to August. When the seedlings are large enough to handle easily, transplant them 2 ft. apart where you want them to flower next year.
Under glass Sow in good seed compost, somewhere warm, from Feb. to March. When there are four leaves, transplant the seedlings 2 ins. apart into boxes of potting compost. To harden them off, put the boxes in a frame or keep them in a sheltered part of the garden by day, taking them in at night in case of frost. Do this for a week or two, then plant them out wherever you want them to flower.

Aster
Ostrich Plume Mixed

Aster Ostrich Plumes have several branches about 2 ft. high with large flowers. The flowers are a mass of curled feathery petals.

The advantage of these Asters is that they flower from mid summer on into autumn when other flowers are over. They are easy to grow in beds or borders and last well as cut flowers.

2 ft.

They come in many different colours like the ones shown.

Asters like well-cultivated soil and open, sunny beds or borders. They are fairly hardy plants which you sow every year (Half Hardy Annual). Sow them in good seed compost under glass in a warm place from March to April. When there are four leaves, transplant the seedlings 2 ins. apart into boxes of potting compost. To harden them off, put the boxes in a frame or keep them in a sheltered part of the garden by day, taking them in at night in case of frost. Do this for a week or two, then plant them out 1½–2 ft. apart in late May or June.

Aster
Single Mixed

The difference between single Asters and other varieties of Asters is their large, golden yellow centre which contrasts vividly with the colours of their petals.

The plants have several stems with one flower each, and grow to 2 ft. Like all Asters, these continue to flower from mid summer into the autumn. They are good for cutting and last well in water.

2 ft.

Here are some of the many colours of Aster, various shades of red, pink, lavender-blue, violet and white.

Single Asters like well-cultivated soil and sun. They are fairly hardy plants which you sow every year (Half Hardy Annual).
Sow them in good seed compost under glass in a warm place from March to April. When there are four leaves, transplant the seedlings 2 ins. apart into boxes of potting compost. To harden them off, put the boxes in a frame or keep them in a sheltered part of the garden by day, taking them in at night in case of frost. Do this for a week or two, then plant them out 12–15 ins. apart in late May or June.

Aubrietia
Springtime
Mixed

Aubrietia is a low plant, spreading out across the ground for 18 ins. or more, in mounds of flowers about 3 ins. high. That is why it is so good between paving stones, on dry walls or rocky banks. It flowers in early summer. The flowers are tiny and delicate, and the leaves have an interesting saw-edged shape.

18 ins.

Here are some of the colours.

Aubrietia like well-drained slightly limey soil and sun or part shade. They are hardy plants and will flower for years (Hardy Perennial).
Sow thinly $\frac{1}{8}$ in. deep in fine soil from April to August. When the seedlings are large enough to handle easily, transplant them at least 2 ft. apart wherever you want them to flower. When they have flowered, cut them back to encourage more flowers next year.
Aubrietia is one of the best plants to grow on small edging walls.

Calendula
Pacific Beauty Mixed

Pacific Beauty Calendulas give you a mixture of bright
and pastel colours. All are double flowers with tightly packed
daisylike petals. The plants
are bushy, 1½-2 ft. high; the
leaves long and narrow.
Calendulas flower all summer long.
They will grow in most soils;
in fact they are one of
the easiest of flowers.
They are good for cutting
and last well in water.

1½-2 ft.

The colours are: yellow, primrose,
apricot and orange.

Calendulas grow in any soil, and do
best in full sun. They are hardy plants
which you sow each year (Hardy
Annuals).
Sow the seeds ¼ in. deep, fairly thinly,
wherever you want them to flower.
When the seedlings come up, thin them
12–18 ins. apart to give them room to
develop. If you want your flowers to
continue into autumn, sow several lots
of calendulas starting at the end of
March till June.
Pluck off any faded heads to help the
plants flower as long as possible.

Canary Creeper
Tropaeolum Canariense

This is a dainty creeper which can easily grow
12 ft. in one season.
It has bright yellow frilly flowers with very
prettily shaped leaves.

Canary Creeper is especially useful for bringing
bright colour to walls, pergolas
and trellises.

Canary Creeper is not fussy about soil, and likes sun or part shade. They are hardy plants which you sow every year (Hardy Annual).

Outdoors Sow in April by putting two seeds in holes, ¼ in. deep and 12 ins. apart, wherever you want them to grow. If both germinate, remove the smaller.

Under glass If you want early flowers, sow the seeds singly, 1–2 ins. apart, in a good seed compost, in March. Keep in a warm place. When there are four leaves, transplant the seedlings 2 ins. apart into boxes of potting compost. Harden the plants off in a cold frame and they will then be ready for planting out in May.

Candytuft
Fairy Mixed

These plants will produce brightly coloured flowers all through the summer. They are only 9 ins. tall, and so are ideal in low growing borders or as edging plants. The flowers, consisting of neatly arranged petals, are about 2 ins. wide.

9 ins.

Here are some of the many colours available.

The seed pods are a particularly interesting shape.

Candytuft likes ordinary well-drained soil with plenty of sun. They are hardy plants which you sow every year (Hardy Annual).
Sow thinly $\frac{1}{8}$ in. deep wherever you want them to flower. You can leave them unthinned if you want a solid mass of colour. If you sow them from the end of March (when the soil has warmed up) through to June, you will have a succession of flowers well into the autumn.
They are ideal in low-growing borders.

Canterbury Bells
All Varieties Mixed

This packet gives you a variety of Canterbury Bells, some single some double. The plants have tall strong stems with several flowers branching out from each. They grow 2-2½ ft. high.

One advantage of Canterbury Bells is that they flower early, well before summer plants begin.

There are many shades of blue, as well as pink and white, available.

2-2½ ft.

Canterbury Bells like good, well-cultivated soil and sun or partial shade. They are hardy plants which you sow one year to flower the next (Hardy Biennial).

Sow thinly outdoors, ¼ in. deep, in May or June, in fine soil in a vacant part of the garden. When the seedlings are 4–6 ins. tall transplant them 6–9 ins. apart in any sunny spot in the back garden. By late Sept. or Oct., the plants will be strong enough to lift and plant 15–18 ins. apart, wherever you want them to flower the following spring. To plant them out, make a hole with a trowel, place the roots in it and press the soil around the roots with your fingers.

Chrysanthemum
Sundance
Annual Mixed

It is easy to see why Chrysanthemums are such favourites with most gardeners. The bright colours and long stems (1-2 ft.) make them equally good as tall border plants or as art flowers for vases or bouquets. Each flower has a separate stem and is a series of rings in contrasting colours.

1-2 ft.

Here are some of the colours of this variety.

Chrysanthemums are easy to grow and they like ordinary soil and sun. They are hardy plants that you sow each year (Hardy Annual).

Sow thinly $\frac{1}{8}$ in. deep wherever you want them to flower. When the seedlings are large enough to handle, thin them 12–15 ins. apart, and replant the ones you've taken out into any gaps that need filling. If you want flowers all summer, sow Chrysanthemums from the end of March (when the soil has warmed up) to the end of May. They may need staking.

Clarkia
Double Mixed

Clarkias are tall plants 2-2½ ft. high. Their long stems are encircled with small double flowers. Because of their height, they are ideal for the centre or back of borders.

Clarkias are very easy to grow. They flower from July to September.

2-2½ ft.

This is how the seeds form just beneath the flower.

The colour range includes white, red, pink, salmon, carmine, mauve and purple.

Clarkias like light, rich soil and sun. They are hardy plants which you sow every year (Hardy Annual).
Sow thinly ⅛ in. deep from March to May in warm moist ground wherever you want them to flower. When the seedlings come up, thin to 6–9 ins. apart to give each plant room to grow and produce the best possible flowers.

Cornflower
Giant Double Blue

Cornflowers are admired for their true blue colour. The flowers are a mass of double petals, the stems long and upright. Because they are 2-3 ft. tall, they look best in the middle or back of borders.

2-3 ft.

Cornflowers are easy to grow and good plants for cutting.

Cornflowers grow in any soil and like sun or part shade. They are hardy plants which you sow every year (Hardy Annual).

Sow fairly thinly $\frac{1}{4}$ in. deep wherever you want them to flower. When the seedlings come up, thin them 12–18 ins. apart so they have room to develop. If you want your flowers to continue into autumn, sow several lots of Cornflowers starting at the end of March till June. Remove any faded heads to help the plants flower as long as possible.

Cosmos
Giant Early Flowering Mixed

Cosmos are like large daisies but have broad petals and fern like leaves. The plants are tall and graceful, 3-4 ft. high. They flower in late summer right through to the first frosts.

Cosmos also look good and last exceptionally well as cut flowers.

3-4 ft.

The colours include dark and light pink, maroon and white.

Cosmos like good fertile soil and sun. They are fairly hardy plants which you sow every year (Half Hardy Annual). Sow in boxes of good seed compost under glass somewhere warm from March to April. When there are four leaves, transplant the seedlings 2 ins. apart into boxes of potting compost. To harden them off, put the boxes in a frame or keep them in a sheltered part of the garden by day, taking them in at night in case of frost. Do this for a week or two, then plant them out $1\frac{1}{2}$–2 ft. apart in late May or June.

Dahlia
Single Bedding Mixed

This is a mixture of large, single
Dahlias which flower from July onwards.
They are easily grown from seed and are
useful both in borders and as cut flowers.

2 ft.

Their large dark green leaves
highlight the flower colours
and also shade the bed below,
an effective way of
discouraging weeds.

Colours include shades of red, yellow,
pink and white.

Dahlias like good fertile soil, and sun or part shade. They are fairly hardy plants and will flower for years (Half Hardy Perennial).

Sow in boxes of seed compost under glass in March. When the seedlings are large enough to handle, transplant them into boxes of compost. Harden them off in a frame for a week or two, then plant them out 2 ft. apart in early June.

When the flowers are over, cut the stems back and take the roots out of the ground and store them over winter in a dry frost-proof place. Then you can replant them the following May.

Daisy
Buttonball
Large Double Flowered Mixed

Buttonball is a large flowered version of the cottage garden
double daisy. The plants are sturdy and compact,
6 ins. high, and produce a mass of flowers all
through the summer.

6 ins.

They are easy to grow in pots, tubs and
window boxes as well as beds and borders.
Buttonball Daisies have clear colours of
red, pink and white.

Double Daisies do well in ordinary well-drained soil and sun. They are hardy plants which you sow one year to flower the next (Hardy Biennial). Sow thinly $\frac{1}{8}$ in. deep in May, June or July. When the seedlings are about 2 ins. tall, transplant them 4–6 ins. apart in any sunny spot.

By late Sept. or Oct. the plants will be strong enough to plant out (6 ins. apart) wherever you want them to flower the following spring.

Delphinium
Summer Spires
Giant Double Mixed

Delphiniums – like Hollyhocks – are tall (5-6 ft.)
graceful plants ideal for the back of beds
and borders. Their tall heads are covered with
double and semi double flowers in all shades of blue,
violet, lavender and white. They flower
for many weeks during the height of summer.

5-6 ft.

Here are some of the
colours available.

Delphiniums like good fertile soil and sun. They are hardy plants and will flower for years (Hardy Perennial).
Outdoors Sow thinly ⅛ in. deep in fine soil in a spare part of the garden from April to August. When the seedlings are 3 ins. tall, plant them out 3 ft. apart wherever you want them to flower next year.
Under glass Sow in boxes of good seed compost from Feb. to March. When there are four leaves, transplant the seedlings 2 ins. apart into boxes of potting compost. Keep them under glass for another two weeks and then harden them off, either by putting the boxes in a frame, or keeping them in a sheltered part of the garden by day, taking them in at night in case of frost. Do this for a week or two, then plant them out wherever you want them to flower.

Dianthus
Annual Pink
Baby Doll

Baby Doll is a garden 'Pink' only 6 ins. high, which flowers from July into autumn. The flowers are single and beautifully marked with contrasting colours; their leaves narrow and pointed.

6 ins.

They look good in tubs and window boxes, rock garden, or beds and borders. Their colours are: rose, white, pink and crimson.

Baby Doll Dianthus like good, well-drained soil and sun. They are fairly hardy plants which you sow each year (Half Hardy Annual).

Outdoors Sow thinly ⅛ in. deep in April or early May wherever you want them to flower. You can leave the plants unthinned, or thin 6 ins. apart when they are 1–2 ins. tall.

Under glass If you want early flowers, sow in good seed compost, somewhere warm, from Feb. to March. When there are four leaves, transplant the seedlings 2 ins. apart into boxes of potting compost. Once they grow big enough to fill the box, harden them off, either by putting the boxes in a frame, or keeping them in a sheltered part of the garden by day, taking them in at night in case of frost. Do this for a week or two, then plant them out wherever you want them to flower.

Forget-Me-Not
Myosotis
Royal Blue

Forget-Me-Nots are very popular and easy to grow. They bloom in late Spring and are lovely either as a solid mass of colour or as companions to wallflowers and tulips which flower at the same time.

6-8 ins.

Forget-Me-Nots are also ideal for window boxes, hanging baskets and tubs.
The flowers are rich blue with distinctive yellow eyes. The plants grow 6-8 ins. tall.

Although they prefer partial shade and a moist soil with a fair amount of organic matter, Forget-Me-Nots will grow almost anywhere. They are sown in the spring of one year to flower the following spring (Hardy Biennial). Sow thinly ⅛ in. deep in fine soil in a seed bed. When the seedlings are about 4 ins. tall, transplant them 9–12 ins. apart in a spare corner of the garden where they can continue to make strong plants. Plant them out in the autumn at least 12 ins. apart wherever you want them to flower.
They are lovely in window boxes with tulips.

Foxglove
Excelsior Hybrids

These Hybrids are one of the best garden Foxgloves because of the size and beauty of their flowers. The neatly arranged tubular flowers grow all round the long (4-5 ft.) strong stems. The plants flower from June to July, and are also excellent for cutting.

4-5 ft.

Their colours are: pink cream, primrose, and purple, all spotted with maroon.

Excelsior Foxgloves need rich, well-cultivated soil. They will grow in sun or shade. They are hardy plants which flower for years (Hardy Perennial). Foxgloves sown outdoors flower the year after you have sown them.
Sow thinly $\frac{1}{8}$ in. deep from April to August. When the seedlings are large enough to handle easily, transplant them 3-4 ft. apart wherever you want them to flower the following June. To plant them out, make a hole with a trowel, place the roots in it and press the soil down and around the roots with your fingers.
When the flowers are over, cut the stems away at the base to stop them seeding.

Godetia
Bush of Beauty
Dwarf Gem Mixed

Godetia is a compact, bushy plant with large densely packed flowers. It flowers all through the summer and in full bloom looks like a brilliant coloured dwarf shrub.

12–15 ins.

There are many colours of Godetia. These are some of them.

Godetia are hardy plants which you sow every year (Hardy Annual). Sow fairly thinly ⅛ in. deep wherever you want them to flower. Thin seedlings 9–12 ins. apart to give them room to develop. If you want your flowers to continue all summer into the autumn, sow several lots of Godetia starting at the end of March till June. Remove any flowers which have faded to help the plants flower as long as possible.

Godetias look particularly good in a border with Dwarf Marigolds and Single Asters.

Gypsophila
Misty Morn
Elegans

Gypsophila is a delicate, graceful bush,
15-18 ins. high, covered with a cloud of
snow white blossom. It flowers all through
the summer. Gypsophila, besides being a
beauty in its own right,
sets off other flowers
to perfection and is
especially lovely
as a cut flower
when arranged
in vases with
Sweet Peas.

15-18 ins.

Gypsophilas like ordinary soil and sun or part shade. They are hardy plants which you sow each year (Hardy Annual).
Sow thinly ⅛ in. deep from the end of March to May wherever you want them to flower. When the seedlings come up, thin them 12-15 ins. apart to give the plants room to develop. You can replant the ones you've taken out into any gaps that need filling.

Helichrysum
Strawflower
Mixed

A valuable plant that provides glorious
colour in the summer.

They grow 2-3 ft. high.

2-3 ft.

The flowers are
made up of rings of
variously coloured petals
(like the ones shown)
around raised centres
which are
often in
contrasting
colours.

You can dry them
for winter arrangements by
hanging them
upside down in a dry
place.

Helichrysum like good fertile soil and
sun. They are fairly hardy plants that
you sow each year (Half Hardy
Annual).
Sow in boxes of good seed compost
under glass for warmth in March or
April. When there are four leaves,
transplant the seedlings 2 ins. apart into
boxes of potting compost. Once they
grow big enough to fill the box, harden
them off either by putting the boxes
in a frame, or keeping them in a
sheltered part of the garden by day,
taking them in at night in case of frost.
Do this for a week or two, then plant
them out $1\frac{1}{2}$–2 ft. apart in late May or
June.

Hollyhock
High Noon
Double Mixed

Hollyhocks are an English garden classic. Their stems six feet high or more, tower over most other flowers with long spikes of big powder puff blooms. They flower year after year, giving a constant show of different colours, like the ones shown.

6 ft.

Hollyhocks like good fertile soil and sun. They are hardy plants which will flower for years (Hardy Perennial).
Outdoors Sow thinly $\frac{1}{8}$ in. deep in fine soil in a spare part of the garden, from April to August. When the seedlings are 3 ins. tall, plant them out 4 ft. apart wherever you want them to flower next year.
Under glass Sow in boxes of good seed compost from Feb. to March. When there are four leaves, transplant the seedlings 2 ins. apart into boxes of potting compost. Keep them under glass for another two weeks and then harden them off, either by putting the boxes in a frame, or keeping them in a sheltered part of the garden by day, taking them in at night in case of frost. Do this for a week or two, then plant them out wherever you want them to flower.
Tie Hollyhocks to stakes if they're likely to be blown over by the wind.

Larkspur
Tall Double-Branching Mixed

Larkspur has small, double flowers growing in long clusters around each of its stems. It belongs to the same family as Delphiniums and looks very like them. Because Larkspur grows 2-3 ft. high, it is best at the back of your border.

2-3 ft.

Larkspur is a good plant for cutting. Here are some of the most popular colours.

Larkspur likes good fertile soil and sun. It is a hardy plant which you sow each year (Hardy Annual).
Sow fairly thinly ⅛ in. deep wherever you want them to flower. When the seedlings come up, thin 12–18 ins. apart to give them room to develop.

If you want your flowers to continue all summer into the autumn, sow several lots of Larkspur starting at the end of March till June.
Remove any flowers which have faded to help the plants flower as long as possible.

Linaria
Fairy Bouquet

Linaria are small bushy plants with clusters of bright flowers which look rather like miniature snapdragons.

9-12 ins.

They flower all summer, and their size (9-12 ins.) and colours make them suitable for beds, borders, tubs, and boxes.

As they are very quick and easy to grow, they are a good flower for children's gardens too.

Here are some of the wide range of colours.

Linarias like rich moist soil and sun. They are hardy plants which you sow each year (Hardy Annual).
Sow thinly $\frac{1}{8}$ in. deep wherever you want them to flower. When the seedlings are 1–2 ins. tall, thin them 6–9 ins. apart. You can replant the ones you take out to fill any gaps elsewhere in the garden. If you want Linarias flowering all summer, sow seed several times, starting at the end of March till the end of May.
To help them flower as long as possible, cut the stems, leaving 3 ins. above the ground, as soon as the flowers fade.

Lobelia
Pendula Sapphire

The flowers are very like the familiar bedding Lobelias, but instead of forming small, bushy clumps, this variety produces long trailing stems, dotted with rich blue flowers with white eyes.

Its trailing growth makes it ideal for hanging baskets, tubs, window-boxes and for growing down banks and walls.

They flower from June right through to the first frosts.

Lobelias like deep, rich soil and sun or part shade. They are fairly hardy plants which you sow each year (Half Hardy Annual).

Sow them in boxes of good seed compost under glass somewhere warm from March to April. When there are four leaves, transplant the seedlings 2 ins. apart into boxes of potting compost. Once they grow big enough to fill the box, harden them off, either by putting the boxes in a frame, or keeping them in a sheltered part of the garden by day, taking them in at night in case of frost. Do this for a week or two, then plant them out 6 ins. apart in late May or June.

They look lovely in hanging baskets with Petunias and Geraniums.

Lobelia
String of Pearls Mixed

These Lobelias have a wide range of colours including red, white, purple and light blue, as well as the familiar dark blue. They grow quickly to form round clumps about 6 ins. high, covered in a mass of tiny flowers, so that few leaves are visible.

6 ins.

Because they flower so long (from June right through to the first frost), Lobelias are popular in both parks and gardens. They are good in tubs, and window boxes, or as edging.

Lobelias like deep, rich soil and sun or part shade. They are fairly hardy plants which you sow each year (Half Hardy Annual).

Sow them in boxes of good seed compost under glass somewhere warm from Feb. to May. When there are four leaves, transplant the seedlings 2 ins. apart into boxes of potting compost. Once they grow big enough to fill the box, harden them off, either by putting the boxes in a frame, or keeping them in a sheltered part of the garden by day, taking them in at night in case of frost. Do this for a week or two, then plant them out 6 ins. apart in late May or June.

They look lovely in window boxes with Petunias.

Lupin
Russell Strain

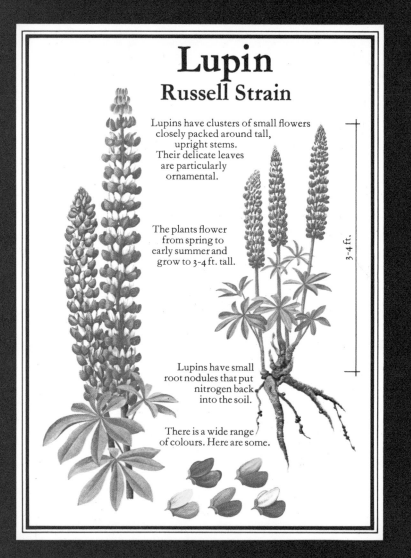

Lupins have clusters of small flowers
closely packed around tall,
upright stems.
Their delicate leaves
are particularly
ornamental.

The plants flower
from spring to
early summer and
grow to 3-4 ft. tall.

3–4 ft.

Lupins have small
root nodules that put
nitrogen back
into the soil.

There is a wide range
of colours. Here are some.

Lupins need deep, rich soil and sun or part shade. They are hardy plants and will flower for years (Hardy Perennial). *Outdoors* Sow the seeds singly in fine soil 3 ins. apart from April to August. when the seedlings are about 4–6 ins. tall, transplant them 3–4 ft. apart wherever you want them to flower. *Under glass* To make sure you get flowers the year you sow them, sow the seeds in good seed compost somewhere warm from Feb. to March. When there are four leaves, transplant the seedlings 2 ins. apart into boxes of potting compost. To harden them off, put the boxes in a frame or keep them in a sheltered part of the garden by day, taking them in at night in case of frost. Do this for a week or two, then plant them out 3–4 ft. apart wherever you want them to flower.

Mesembryanthemum
Livingstone Daisy
Criniflorum Mixed

3 ins.

Mesembryanthemum has a mass
of daisylike flowers which come out
from June to August.
It grows very close to the ground,
only 3 ins. high, so is best for
rock gardens, banks or the edges
of borders – also tubs and
window boxes.

Mesembryanthemum flowers come
in many bright colours with paler
centres, like the ones shown.

Mesembryanthemum will grow in any
soil but needs a place that is dry and
sunny. It is a fairly hardy plant which
you sow each year (Half Hardy
Annual).
Sow somewhere warm in good seed
compost under glass from March to
April. When there are four leaves,
transplant the seedlings 2 ins. apart
into boxes of potting compost. To
harden them off, put the boxes in a
frame or keep them in a sheltered part
of the garden by day, taking them in at
night in case of frost. Do this for a
week or two, then plant them out 9 ins.
apart in late May or June.

Mignonette
Sweet Scented

Mignonette has a fragrant perfume that few
plants can equal. A few seeds sown here and there
between other plants will give flowers
that will scent the whole garden.

12 ins.

A few seeds sown indoors
in a pot will bring the fragrance
of the summer border
into the house.

Mignonettes like moist soil and shade.
They are hardy plants which you sow
each year (Hardy Annual).
Sow a few seeds in March or April ⅛ in.
deep in spaces between other plants
in the flower bed. When the seedlings
are 1–2 ins. tall, thin them 4–6 ins.
apart to give the plants room to
develop.

Indoors You can also grow them
indoors by sowing 4 or 6 seeds in 4–5
in. pots (filled with good soil or
potting compost). Keep the pots
watered well and in a window where
they will get sun for only part of the
day.

Morning Glory
Ipomoea
Heavenly Blue

Morning Glories are known for their true blue, trumpet shaped flowers which open in the mornings and are shut by the afternoon.

The plants climb to 8 ft. or more and have twining stems and heart shaped leaves.

They bloom continuously from July to Sept., producing flowers up to 5 ins. across.

You can train them up a fence or wall, or on sticks or canes if you grow them in pots.

8 ft.

Morning Glories need rich, fertile soil and a sunny sheltered place. They are fairly hardy plants which you sow each year (Half Hardy Annual).

Soak the seeds in water for 24 hours to help them start growing.

Sow them in good seed compost under glass, somewhere warm, from March to April. When there are four leaves, transplant the seedlings, singly, into 3 in. pots or plant them out in June, when the weather is really warm. When they get too big for the 3 in. pots, put them into 8–10 in. pots which you can move to any sunny sheltered place in the garden.

Support the plants with sticks or canes, or train them up a trellis, fence or wall. You can tie them with string or use wire rings.

Nasturtium
Little Beauty
Dwarf Mixed

These bright flowers will grow in almost any poor dry soil. They are ideal plants for window boxes, tubs and pots, and for children's gardens too.

9-12 ins.

The seeds can be used in cooking and young leaves can be used in salads.

Here are some of the colours available.

Nasturtiums thrive in poor, dry soil with plenty of sun. They are hardy plants which you sow each year (Hardy Annual).

The young seedlings are tender and can easily be damaged by frost, so sow from mid-April to June and this will give you flowers right through to the autumn.

Sow the seeds $\frac{1}{2}$ in. deep and 6 ins. apart wherever you want them to flower. When the seedlings come up, thin them 12–18 ins. apart to give them room to develop.

They look lovely in hanging baskets with trailing Lobelias and Cascade Petunias. Grow them in window boxes on their own for a superb show of colour.

Nasturtium
Giant Climbing Mixed

A vigorous climbing variety of Nasturtium which, if you tie the plants as they grow, can be trained 10 ft. up trellises and fences, or left to ramble down garden banks. The great advantage of these plants is that they produce a wealth of colour on poor, dry soil, where others may find it difficult to grow at all. You can use the small caper like seeds for cooking and the young leaves can be used to add spice to salads.

10 ft.

This variety has many shades of colour ranging from bright yellow to clear red.

Nasturtiums thrive in poor, dry soil with plenty of sun. If you put them in rich soil, you get far too many leaves and hardly any flowers. They are hardy plants which you sow each year (Hardy Annual).

The young seedlings are tender and can easily be damaged by frost, so sow from mid-April to June and this will give you flowers right through to the autumn.

Sow the seeds $\frac{1}{2}$ in. deep and 6 ins. apart wherever you want them to flower. When the seedlings come up, thin them 12–18 ins. apart to give them room to develop.

Nasturtium
Gleam Hybrids

The great advantage about these plants is that they produce a wealth of colour on poor, dry soil, where others may find it difficult to grow at all. They grow 9-12 ins. tall.
You can use the small caper like seeds for cooking and the young leaves can be used to add spice to salads.

9-12 ins.

Here are some of the bright yellows and reds available.

Nasturtiums thrive in poor, dry soil with plenty of sun. They are hardy plants which you sow each year (Hardy Annual).
The young seedlings are tender and can easily be damaged by frost, so sow from mid-April to June and this will give you flowers right through to the autumn.

Sow the seeds $\frac{1}{2}$ in. deep and 6 ins. apart wherever you want them to flower. When the seedlings come up, thin them 12–18 ins. apart to give them room to develop.
Nasturtiums are ideal for window boxes, tubs and pots, and for children's gardens too. They look lovely in hanging baskets with trailing Lobelias.

Nemesia
Carnival Mixed

Nemesias are bushy plants 9-12 ins. high each one a mass of flowers. They look best grown massed in beds, tubs or window boxes. The advantage of Nemesias is that they grow and flower very quickly and last all through the summer.

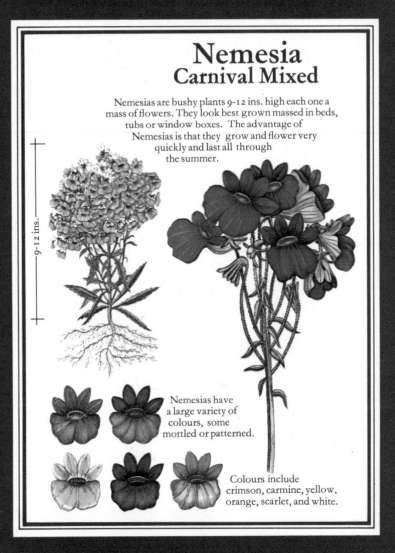

9-12 ins.

Nemesias have a large variety of colours, some mottled or patterned.

Colours include crimson, carmine, yellow, orange, scarlet, and white.

Nemesias like rich, well-drained soil and full sun. They are fairly hardy plants which you sow every year (Half Hardy Annual).

Outdoors Sow thinly ⅛ in. deep in April or early May wherever you want the plants to grow. You can leave them unthinned or thin to 6–9 ins. apart when the seedlings are big enough to handle easily.

Under glass If you want early flowers, sow in good seed compost somewhere warm in Feb. or March. When there are four leaves, transplant the seedlings 2 ins. apart into boxes of potting compost. Once they grow big enough to fill the box, harden them off, either by putting the boxes in a frame, or keeping them in a sheltered part of the garden by day, taking them in at night in case of frost. Do this for a week or two, then plant out 6–9 ins. apart wherever you want them to flower.

Nemophila
Baby Blue Eyes

The advantage of Nemophila is that it will
grow almost anywhere. From June to Aug. it is a mass of clear
blue flowers with white centres and feathery, light green leaves.

6 ins.

It is a bushy plant, only 6 ins. high,
perfect for window boxes as well
as in the garden.

Nemophila does well in any soil, but
thrives in a moist soil and shade. It is
a hardy plant that you sow every year
(Hardy Annual).
Sow thinly ⅛ in. deep wherever you
want them to flower. When the seedlings are 1–2 ins. tall, thin them 6 ins.
apart. If you want your flowers to continue all summer, sow several lots of
Nemophila starting at the end of
March till June.

Nicotiana
Sensation Hybrids

Unlike some Nicotiana varieties, this Hybrid has flowers that remain open all day.
It is a tall plant (2-3 ft.) with compact blooms and a wide variety of colours.

2-3 ft.

Sensation Hybrids are very effective planted in clumps in the centre of borders or among shrubs. Colours include white, cream, pink, crimson and yellow.

Nicotianas like good, fertile soil and sun or part shade. They are fairly hardy plants that you sow each year (Half Hardy Annual).
Sow in boxes of good seed compost under glass somewhere warm in March or April. When there are four leaves, transplant the seedlings 2 ins. apart into boxes of potting compost. Once they grow big enough to fill the box, harden them off either by putting the boxes in a frame, or keeping them in a sheltered part of the garden by day, taking them in at night in case of frost. Do this for a week or two, then plant them out 12–15 ins. apart in late May or June, ready for flowering.

Nigella
Love-in-a-mist
Persian Jewels

Nigella flowers almost the whole season through
from early summer to the first frosts. Not only
does it make a very pretty cut flower,
but in the garden its dainty flowers
and fine leaves add a touch of delicacy
to the border.

15–18 ins.

It is very
easy to grow and is
very suitable for
children's gardens.

Colours include
pale and dark blue, white, rose and pink,
and its seed pods are an interesting shape.

Nigellas like ordinary soil and sun or part shade. They are hardy plants which you sow each year (Hardy Annual).
Sow ⅛ in. deep, fairly thinly, wherever you want them to flower. When the seedlings come up, thin them 6–9 ins. apart to give the plants room to develop and flower.

Pansy
Choice Mixed

Pansies are loved for their velvet texture and rich colours.
They are spreading plants, 6 ins. high, with many flowers and tapered leaves.

Pansies go on flowering from May right through to Sept. They are excellent for beds, borders, tubs, and window boxes, and also good plants for cutting.

6 ins.

The colour range is wide and includes the ones shown here.

Pansies like rich, deep soil and sun or part shade. They are hardy plants and will flower for years, but you get bigger and better flowers if you sow new seeds every year, and if you pick off the seed heads the plants will flower longer (Hardy Perennial treated as Half Hardy Annual).
Outdoors Sow thinly $\frac{1}{8}$ in. deep in March or April. When the seedlings are large enough to handle easily, thin them 6 ins. apart.

Under glass If you want early flowers, sow in good seed compost somewhere warm from Feb. to March. When there are four leaves, transplant the seedlings 2 ins. apart into boxes of potting compost. To harden them off, put the boxes in a frame or keep them in a sheltered part of the garden by day, taking them in at night in case of frost. Do this for a week or two, then plant them out 6–9 ins. apart wherever you want them to flower.

Petunia
Fanfare
Fine Mixed

The great thing about Petunias is that they go on and on flowering to give you a splash of colour from June right through to the autumn. The flowers are trumpet shaped; the plants bushy, 15-18 ins. tall with leaves growing all the way up their stems. Petunias are easy to grow in window boxes as well as in beds and borders.

15-18 ins.

The colours are: white, pink, rose, red, purple, pale and dark blue.

Petunias like good, fertile soil and sun. They are fairly hardy plants which you sow each year (Half Hardy Annual). Sow in good seed compost under glass somewhere warm from March to April. When there are four leaves, transplant the seedlings 2 ins. apart into boxes of potting compost. To harden them off, put the boxes in a frame or keep them in a sheltered part of the garden by day, taking them in at night in case of frost. Do this for a week or two, then plant them out 12 ins. apart in late May or June.

Pinch off any faded heads to help the plants flower as long as possible. They look lovely in window boxes with trailing Lobelias.

Phacelia
Campanularia

These plants have
beautiful bell-shaped
deep gentian-blue
flowers and are very
easy to grow. They flower from June to Sept.
The plants are low (9 ins.) and bushy,
so they look lovely as edging for beds and
borders, or in a rock garden.
They can also be grown as a pot plant
for indoors.

9 ins.

Phacelia like good, well-dug soil and need plenty of sun. They are hardy plants which you sow each year (Hardy Annual).
Sow thinly $\frac{1}{8}$ in. deep wherever you want them to flower. When the seedlings are 1–2 ins. high, thin them 6 ins. apart to give the plants room to develop and flower.

Phlox
Annual Mixed

Phlox have big clusters of open flowers in many different
colours, each with a clearly marked centre. They grow on
upright stems about 1 ft. high and flower in plenty
from July to Sept. Phlox do well in tubs and window
boxes as well as in beds
and borders. They look good
and last well as cut flowers.

1 ft.

The colours are: rose,
salmon, scarlet,
crimson, primrose, white
and various blues.

Phlox like good, fertile soil and sun.
They are fairly hardy plants which you
sow each year (Half Hardy Annual).
Sow in boxes of good seed compost,
under glass, somewhere warm from
March to April. When there are four
leaves, transplant the seedlings 2 ins.
apart into boxes of potting compost.
Once they grow big enough to fill the
box, harden them off, either by putting
the boxes in a frame, or keeping them
in a sheltered part of the garden by day,
taking them in at night in case of frost.
Do this for a week or two, then plant
them out 9–12 ins. apart in late May or
June.
Pick off any faded heads to help the
plants flower as long as possible.

Polyanthus
Finest Mixed

Polyanthus plants belong to the same family as primroses and are very like them, but the flowers are larger, have many colours and grow in clusters on sturdy upright stems.
They flower in spring and early summer and grow to 9 ins.

9 ins.

These are some of the many colours of Polyanthus.

Polyanthus like moist, fertile soil and sun or part shade. They are hardy plants which flower for years (Hardy Perennial).

Outdoors Sow thinly in May in frames or open ground and cover them very lightly. By Sept. they will be ready to plant out, 9–12 ins. apart, wherever you want them to flower.

Under glass Sow in boxes or pots of good seed compost from Feb. to March. Leave them uncovered or just cover them very lightly with a little coarse sand. When the seedlings are large enough to handle, transplant them 2 ins. apart into boxes of potting compost. Keep them under glass for another two weeks. Then put them into a frame or in a warm sheltered part of the garden. In Sept. you can plant them wherever you want them to flower the following year.

You can grow Polyanthus indoors in pots.

Californian Poppy
Eschscholzia
Hybrids

Every part of the Californian Poppy –
leaf, stem, flower – is delicately formed
and adds a touch of elegance
to beds and borders.

12-15 ins

They are very simple to grow and this,
together with their bright colours, make
them ideal for children to grow in their
part of the garden.

Colours include shades of orange,
sunny yellow, pink and cream.
They grow 12-15 ins. high.

Californian Poppies like ordinary soil
and sun. They are hardy plants which
you sow each year (Hardy Annual).
Sow fairly thinly $\frac{1}{8}$ in. deep between the
end of March and May wherever they
are to flower. When the seedlings
come up, thin them 6–9 ins. apart to
give the flowers plenty of room to
develop.

Iceland Poppy
Mixed

This mixture of Iceland Poppies gives you many different colours. The flowers are large and rise elegantly on slender yet firm stems well above their leaves, which encircle the base of the plant.

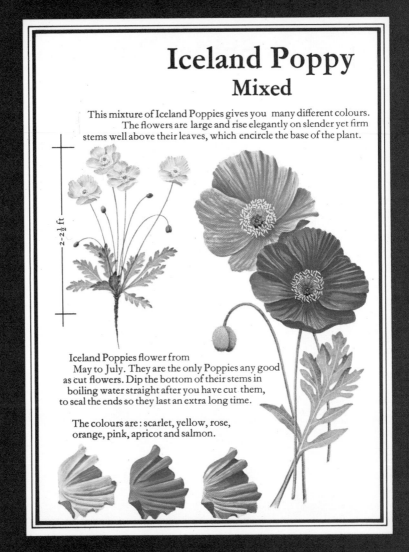

2–2½ ft

Iceland Poppies flower from May to July. They are the only Poppies any good as cut flowers. Dip the bottom of their stems in boiling water straight after you have cut them, to seal the ends so they last an extra long time.

The colours are: scarlet, yellow, rose, orange, pink, apricot and salmon.

Iceland Poppies like rich, fertile soil and sun. They are hardy plants which you sow one year to flower the next (Hardy Biennial).
Sow thinly in fine soil in a vacant part of the garden from April to July. When the plants are 3–4 ins. tall, transplant them 6 ins. apart in a similar position. By Sept. or Oct. they will be strong enough to plant 1½–2 ft. apart wherever you want them to flower next May.

Shirley Poppy
Single Mixed

Shirley Poppies have large, single flowers in many colours, both bright and soft – some a blend of two colours. The plants are strong with graceful yet firm stems and fern-shaped, soft green leaves. They are easy to grow and flower all summer long.

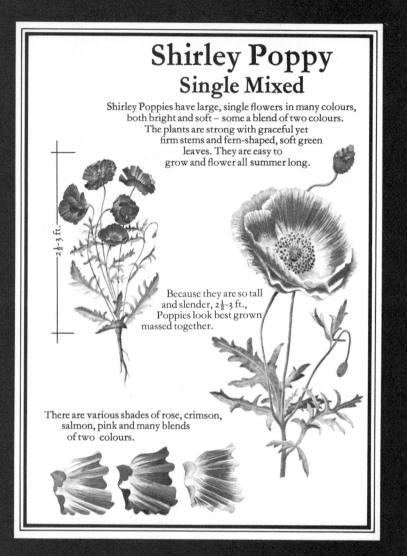

Because they are so tall and slender, 2½-3 ft., Poppies look best grown massed together.

There are various shades of rose, crimson, salmon, pink and many blends of two colours.

Shirley Poppies will grow in any soil, but like sun. They are hardy plants which you sow each year (Hardy Annual).

Sow thinly ⅛ in. deep wherever you want them to flower. When the seedlings are large enough to handle, thin them 1½–2 ft. apart. You can replant the ones you take out to fill any gaps. If you want your flowers to continue into autumn, sow several lots of Poppies starting at the end of March till June.

Pyrethrum
Single Mixed

Pyrethrums look like large Daisies with big yellow centres
and beautifully coloured petals. They grow
2 ft. high on strong stems above delicate feathery leaves.
Pyrethrums look good as cut flowers and as
border plants. They last well in water.

2 ft.

There are
various shades of
scarlet, rose, pink, cherry red,
crimson and pure white.

Pyrethrums like good rich soil and sun
or part shade. They are hardy plants
which flower for years (Hardy Perennial). Pyrethrums sown outdoors
flower the year after you have sown
them. To flower the same year, you
have to sow them under glass.
Outdoors Sow thinly in fine soil, in a
spare part of the garden, from May to
June. When the seedlings are 1–2 ins.
high, transplant them 6 ins. apart, and
then plant out 1½ ft. apart wherever
you want them to flower in autumn.

Under glass Sow in boxes of good seed
compost somewhere warm from Feb.
to March. When there are four leaves,
transplant the seedlings 2 ins. apart into
boxes of potting compost. Once they
grow big enough to fill the box, harden
them off, either by putting the boxes in
a frame or keeping them in a sheltered
part of the garden by day, taking them
in at night in case of frost. Do this
for a week or two, then plant them out
2 ft. apart wherever you want them to
flower.

Schizanthus
Butterfly Flower Mixed

Schizanthus have clusters of single flowers which look
like small, exotic orchids. Their centres are spotted
with yellow and gold.
The plants are bushy 1½-2 ft. high, with fern-like leaves.

They flower from June to Oct. in window boxes
or in the garden, and make beautiful pot plants as well.

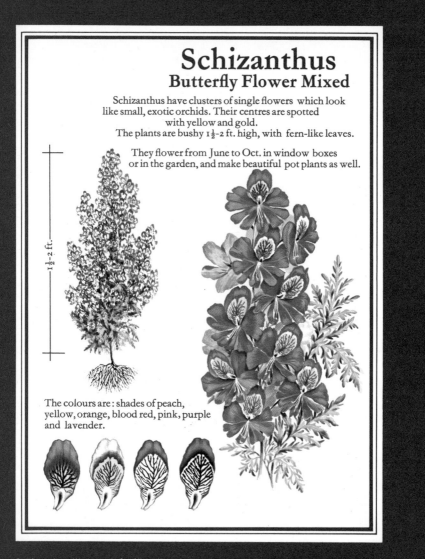

1½-2 ft.

The colours are: shades of peach,
yellow, orange, blood red, pink, purple
and lavender.

Schizanthus like good, fertile soil and
sun. They are fairly hardy plants which
you sow every year (Half Hardy
Annual).
Outdoors Sow in April and May ⅛ in.
deep. When the seedlings are 1–2 ins.
tall, thin them 12 ins. apart.
Under glass Sow in good seed compost
somewhere warm from March to April.
When there are four leaves, put the
seedlings 2 ins. apart into boxes of
potting compost. Once they grow big

enough to fill the box, harden them off,
either by putting the boxes in a frame,
or keeping them in a sheltered part of
the garden by day, taking them in at
night in case of frost. Do this for a week
or two, then plant them out in late May
or June.
If you want Schizanthus as house-
plants, put them singly into 4–5 in.
pots of potting compost when the
young plants are 6–8 ins. tall.

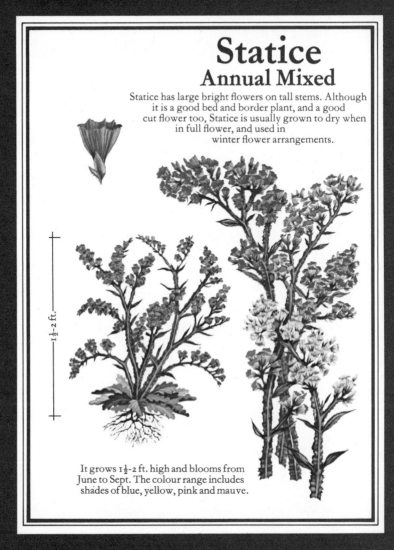

Statice
Annual Mixed

Statice has large bright flowers on tall stems. Although
it is a good bed and border plant, and a good
cut flower too, Statice is usually grown to dry when
in full flower, and used in
winter flower arrangements.

$1\frac{1}{2}$-2 ft.

It grows $1\frac{1}{2}$-2 ft. high and blooms from
June to Sept. The colour range includes
shades of blue, yellow, pink and mauve.

Statice like rich, well-dug soil and
plenty of sun. They are fairly hardy
plants which you sow each year (Half
Hardy Annual).
The seeds are inside dried flower heads
which you press into boxes of good
seed compost in Feb. or March, and
then cover with soil and keep under
glass. When the seedlings are 1–2 ins.
tall, transplant them 2 ins. apart
into boxes of potting compost. Once

they grow big enough to fill the box,
harden them off, either by putting the
boxes in a frame, or keeping them in a
sheltered part of the garden by day,
taking them in at night in case of frost.
Do this for a week or two, then plant
them out $1\frac{1}{2}$–2 ft. apart in May or June.
Drying Cut the flowers when they look
at their best, and hang them in bunches
anywhere airy until they are completely
dry.

Night Scented Stock

This variety of stock opens its pale purple flowers at night, when its heady scent floats on the air. Sow some near your windows to enjoy the sweet scent coming in on summer evenings.

Night Scented Stock is a bushy plant with 4-petalled flowers and long, narrow, grey-green leaves. It flowers in summer and grows 9-12 ins. tall. As the flowers are shut during the day, and so a bit dull, it's a good idea to mix the contents of the packet with seed of Virginian Stock, which gives you plenty of colour during the day.

9-12 ins.

Night Scented Stock grows in any soil and does not need sun. It is a hardy plant which you sow each year (Hardy Annual).

Sow fairly thinly $\frac{1}{8}$ in. deep wherever you want them to flower. It is best to leave Night Scented Stock unthinned. The thicker it grows the stronger its fragrance. If you want your flowers to continue into autumn, sow several lots of Night Scented Stock starting at the end of March till June.

If you grow it in window boxes with Virginian Stock, you get fragrance as well as colour.

Ten Week Stock
Dwarf Finest Mixed

The plants grow 12-15 ins. tall, with stems which are covered with closely packed flowers that begin to open ten weeks after the seeds were sown (hence the name).
The flowers are mostly double but some singles may be produced.

In the old cottage gardens they were known as Stock Gillyflowers and were prized for the subtle scent that surrounds them and for their lovely soft colours.

There is a wide range of colours including scarlet, cream, yellow, purple, peach and shades of blue.

These Stocks like rich, well-dug soil with a trace of lime, and sun or part shade. They are fairly hardy plants that you sow each year (Half Hardy Annual).

Sow in boxes of good seed compost, under glass for warmth, in March or April. When there are four leaves, transplant the seedlings 2 ins. apart into boxes of potting compost. Once they grow big enough to fill the box, harden them off, either by putting the boxes in a frame, or keeping them in a sheltered part of the garden by day, taking them in at night in case of frost. Do this for a week or two, then plant them out 6–9 ins. apart in late May or June.

Virginian Stock
Finest Mixed

Virginian Stock has a mass of colourful four petalled flowers on slender stems. The plants are bushy, 9-12 ins. high, and flower all through the summer. Virginian Stock is a very easy plant to grow and will do well in most soils.

9-12 ins.

The colours are: white, yellow and various shades of red.

Virginian Stock will grow in any soil and does best in sun or part shade. It is a hardy plant which you sow each year (Hardy Annual).

Sow fairly thinly $\frac{1}{8}$ in. deep wherever you want them to flower. It is best to leave the seedlings unthinned. The thicker they grow, the more flowers you get. If you want your flowers to continue into autumn, sow several lots of seeds starting at the end of March till June. The flowers come out four weeks after you have sown them, and last a long time.

Virginian Stock grows well in window boxes. If you mix with Night Scented Stock, you get fragrance as well as colour.

Sunflower
Tall Single

These Sunflowers can grow blooms 1 ft. across and more, with large centres of purple and brown. They grow easily 7-8 ft. high, and with a little extra care will reach 14 ft. and more.

8 ft.

These superb Sunflowers continue to flower from late July to Sept. If you cut and dry the heads when they finish flowering, the seeds can be eaten or used as pet food for budgerigars, hamsters or white mice.

Sunflowers like good, well-cultivated soil and full sun. They are hardy plants which you sow each year (Hardy Annual).

If you want your Sunflowers to grow as high as possible, dig the soil well, adding some organic manure before sowing. Also make sure your flowers have plenty of space and sun.

Sow thinly ½ in. deep wherever you want them to flower. When the seedlings are 1–2 ins. tall, thin them 4–5 ft. apart. If you want your flowers to continue into autumn, sow several lots of Sunflowers starting at the end of March till the end of May.

Support Sunflowers by tying them to canes or strong sticks.

Sweet Pea
Giant Waved

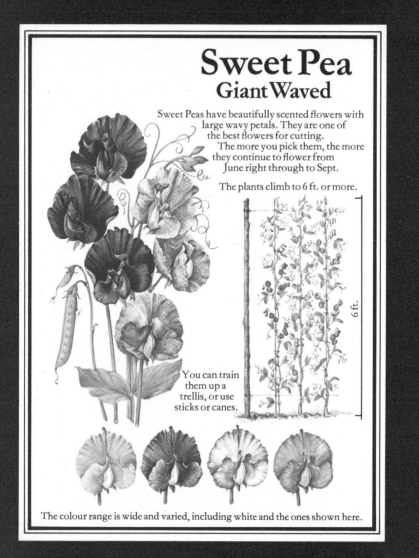

Sweet Peas have beautifully scented flowers with large wavy petals. They are one of the best flowers for cutting. The more you pick them, the more they continue to flower from June right through to Sept.

The plants climb to 6 ft. or more.

6 ft.

You can train them up a trellis, or use sticks or canes.

The colour range is wide and varied, including white and the ones shown here.

Sweet Peas are hardy plants which you sow each year (Hardy Annual).

To help the seeds start to grow, nick the seed-coat or soak them overnight in tepid water.

Outdoors Sow the seeds 6 ins. apart in rows 1 in. deep from March to May, wherever you want them to flower, and thin to 12 ins. apart later.

Under glass Sow the seeds singly, $\frac{1}{4}$ in. deep, in 3 in. pots of good seed com-post, somewhere warm, in Oct. or Jan./Feb. Harden them off and then plant out in April wherever you want them to flower. When there are four pairs of leaves, pinch out the tips of the seedlings to encourage side shoots and more flowers.

Support the plants by tying them up frequently. Sweet Peas are hungry plants. During May and June they like a weekly feed of liquid manure.

Sweet Scabious
Fine Mixed

Sweet Scabious are easy to grow and flower all through
the summer. The long stems, (2½ ft.) carry several bright
flowers and they are excellent as cut flowers because
they last a long time in water. The dried seed heads
are useful for winter arrangements too.

2-2½ ft.

Sweet Scabious has a wide range of colours
including shades of blue, lavender,
crimson, pink, cerise, maroon and white.
Here are some of them.

Sweet Scabious like rich, well-dug soil
and need plenty of sun. They are fairly
hardy plants that you sow each year
(Half Hardy Annual).

Outdoors Sow ⅛ in. deep in April or
early May wherever you want them to
flower. When the seedlings are 1–2 ins.
tall, thin them 1½ ft. apart to give the
flowers plenty of room to develop.

Under glass If you want early flowers,
sow in boxes of good seed compost
somewhere warm in Feb. or March.
When there are four leaves, transplant
the seedlings 2 ins. apart into boxes of
potting compost. Once they grow big
enough to fill the box, harden them off,
either by putting the boxes in a frame,
or keeping them in a sheltered part of
the garden by day, taking them in at
night in case of frost. Do this for a week
or two, then plant them out 1½ ft. apart
wherever you want them to flower.

Sweet Sultan
Large Flowered Mixed

These are old favourites of the cottage garden. They have
large sweetly scented double flowers which resemble huge
Cornflowers, and grow up to 2 ft. high.
They are very easy to grow, and look best
in the middle or back of borders. They are
also good as cut flowers,
because they last well in water.

2 ft.

Here are some of
the colours available.

Sweet Sultans will grow in any soil,
but they need sun. They are hardy
plants that you sow each year (Hardy
Annual).
Sow thinly $\frac{1}{8}$ in. deep wherever you
want them to flower. When the seedlings are 1–2 ins. high, thin them
12–18 ins. apart to give them room to
develop. You can replant the ones you
take out into another part of the garden
that needs more flowers. If you sow
some seeds several times between the
end of March and the end of May,
you will have flowers one after another
all summer.

Sweet William
Large Flowered
Mixed

Sweet Williams have bunches of flat open flowers, single and double. Their colours are particularly bright.
The plants flower in June and July; they grow $1\frac{1}{2}$-2 ft. and are good for cutting. Their sweet scented flowers last a long time, both indoors and out.

$1\frac{1}{2}$-2 ft.

The colour range is wide and includes the ones shown here.

Sweet Williams like good, well-dug soil and sun or part shade. They are hardy plants which you sow one year to flower the next (Hardy Biennial). Sow thinly $\frac{1}{4}$ in. deep outdoors in May or June. When the seedlings are 4 6 ins. tall, transplant them 6–9 ins. apart into any sunny spot. By late Sept. or Oct. the plants will be bushy and strong enough to lift and plant wherever you want them to flower the following spring.

Verbena
Rainbow Mixed

Verbenas are ever popular garden flowers in an assortment
of bright colours that bloom all through the summer.
The primrose shaped flowers grow in dense clusters
9-12 ins. high, so they are good for window boxes and tubs.
They have a soft summery fragrance.
One advantage of these flowers is
that they will stand up
well to wet weather.

9-12 ins.

Here are some
of the wide range
of colours.

Verbenas like good, fertile soil and
plenty of sun. They are fairly hardy
plants that you sow each year (Half
Hardy Annual).

Sow in boxes of good seed compost,
under glass for warmth, in March or
April. When there are four leaves,
transplant the seedlings 2 ins. apart
into boxes of potting compost. Once
they grow high enough to fill the box,
harden them off, either by putting the
boxes in a frame, or keeping them in
a sheltered part of the garden by day,
taking them in at night in case of frost.
Do this for a week or two, then plant
them out 9-12 ins. apart in late May or
June wherever you want them to
flower.

To keep Verbenas flowering all
summer, cut off the flower heads as
as soon as they fade.

Viola
Choice Mixed

Violas are rich, velvety flowers. Some have centres marked
with strong blotches,
others with delicate thin lines.
They are compact plants,
only 6 ins. high, which flower
in plenty from July through
to the first frosts, and are good
for beds and cutting.

6 ins.

Their colours are: purple, mauve,
lilac, dark red, yellow and cream
with various coloured markings.

Violas need rich, deep soil and sun or
part shade. They are hardy and will
flower for years (Hardy Perennial
treated as a Half Hardy Annual), but
you get the best flowers if you sow new
seeds each year.
Outdoors Sow thinly ⅛ in. deep in June
and July. When the seedlings are 1–2
ins. tall, transplant them 6 ins. apart,
and plant them out in autumn
wherever you want them to flower.
Under glass If you want flowers the first
year, sow in good seed compost somewhere warm from Feb. to March.
When there are four leaves, transplant
the seedlings 2 ins. apart into boxes of
potting compost. Once they grow big
enough to fill the box, harden them off,
either by putting the boxes in a frame,
or keeping them in a sheltered part of
the garden by day, taking them in at
night in case of frost. Do this for a week
or two, then plant them out 6–9 ins.
apart wherever you want them to
flower.

Viscaria
Mixed

Viscaria, sometimes known as Campion, is a colourful and easy to grow flower, useful both for borders and cut flowers (15-18 ins. high).
Viscaria is a delicate looking plant which blooms all summer, with sprays of flowers above bright green leaves.

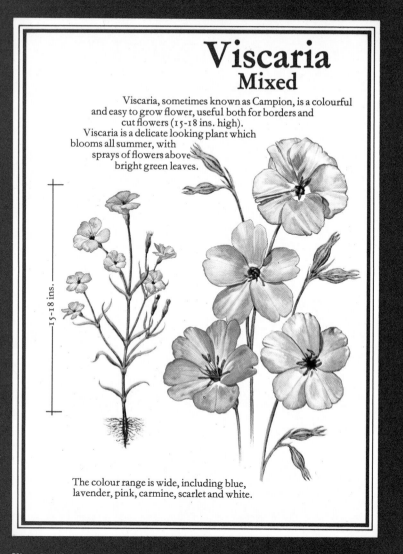

15-18 ins.

The colour range is wide, including blue, lavender, pink, carmine, scarlet and white.

Viscarias like ordinary soil and sun. They are hardy plants which you sow each year (Hardy Annual).
Sow thinly ⅛ in. deep any time between the end of March and the end of May, wherever you want them to flower.

When the seedlings are 1–2 ins. tall, thin them 12–15 ins. apart, to give the plants room to develop. You can replant the ones you have taken out into any gaps that need filling.

Wallflower
Large Flowered Mixed

Here is a varied mixture of Wallflowers in a wide range of white, yellows, oranges and reds. Each plant carries several stems with clusters of strong scented flowers ideal for massed colour and scent in beds, borders or window boxes.

15-18 ins.

They flower from May to June, and grow 15-18 ins. high.

Wallflowers do well in ordinary, well-drained soil and sun. They are hardy plants which you sow one year to flower the next (Hardy Biennial). Sow the seeds thinly outdoors, ¼ in. deep, in May or June. When the seedlings are 4–6 ins. tall, transplant them 6–9 ins. apart in any sunny spot. Pinch out the growing tip to help the plants become bushy. By late Sept. or Oct. the plants will be strong enough to plant wherever you want them to flower the following spring. To plant them out, make a hole with a trowel, place the roots in it and press the soil down firmly round the roots with your fingers.

Zinnia
Mammoth Mixed

This is the largest flowered variety of Zinnias.
The flowers have big petals in bright colours.
Although this variety is quite tall (2-2½ ft.), the plants
are bushy and full-leaved and each
bears several flowers.

2 -2½ ft.

Zinnias are ideal as
a mixed border or
for massed colour in
beds. They are
good cut flowers too.
The colour range is
wide including yellow,
salmon, pink, scarlet,
orange and purple.

Here are some of them.

Zinnias like rich, fertile soil and plenty of sun. They are fairly hardy plants which you sow each year (Half Hardy Annual).
Outdoors Sow thinly ¼ in. deep in May wherever you want the plants to grow. When the seedlings are 1–2 ins. tall, thin them 2 ft. apart. You can replant the ones you have taken out elsewhere in the garden into any gaps that need filling.
Under glass If you want early flowers, sow in good seed compost somewhere warm in March. When there are four leaves, transplant the seedlings 2 ins. apart into boxes of potting compost. Once they grow big enough to fill the box, harden them off, either by putting the boxes in a frame, or keeping them in a sheltered part of the garden by day, taking them in at night in case of frost. Do this for a week or two, then plant them out 2 ft. apart in late May or June, wherever you want them to flower. Pick off any faded heads to help the plants flower as long as possible.

Table of Sowing and Flowering Times

Name	Sowing	Flowering	Remarks
Perennials			
Alyssum Saxatile Gold Dust	April – August outdoors; Feb. – March under glass	March – April	Good for edging banks, rockeries
Aquilegia Columbine	April – August outdoors; Feb. – March under glass	May – June	Graceful early flowers for borders
Aubrietia Rock Cress	April – August outdoors	April – May	Forms neat mounds. Edging, banks, rockeries
Dahlia	March under glass	July – Oct.	Only half hardy; store in frost-free place in winter
Delphinium	April – August outdoors; Feb. – March under glass	July – August	Fine border plant
Foxglove Digitalis	April – August outdoors	June	Effective in light shade under trees
Hollyhock Althaea	April – August outdoors; Feb. – March under glass	July – August	Back of border or to hide fence
Lupin	April – August outdoors; Feb. – March under glass	June – July	Handsome border plant
Pansy	March – April outdoors; Feb. – March under glass		Edging, bedding, under-planting shrubs
Polyanthus	May outdoors; Feb. – March under glass	April – May	Edging, bedding, under-planting shrubs

Plant	Sowing	Flowering	Use
Pyrethrum	May – June outdoors; Feb. – March under glass	June – July	Pretty plant for borders and cutting
Viola	June – July outdoors; Feb. – March under glass	July – Oct.	Ideal for carpet and under-planting
Biennials			
Canterbury Bells Campanula medium	May – June outdoors	June	Will make handsome border groups
Double Flowered Daisy Bellis perennis flore pleno	May – July outdoors	March – May	Pretty spring bedding and edging
Forget-Me-Not Myosotis	April – May outdoors	March – May	Ideal for under-planting shrubs, bulbs, roses
Iceland Poppy Papaver nudicaule	April – July outdoors	May – July	Bright colour for sunny border
Sweet William Dianthus barbatus	May – June outdoors	June – July	Ideal cut flowers or groups in borders
Wallflower Cheiranthus	May – June outdoors	May – June	Popular spring bedding
Annuals			
Alyssum	April – May outdoors; Feb. – March under glass	June – Sept.	Ideal carpet, edging or under-planting
Antirrhinum Snapdragon	April – May outdoors; Feb. – March under glass	June – Oct.	Good summer bedding or groups in borders

Name	Sowing	Flowering	Remarks
Annuals			
Aster Ostrich Plume	March – April under glass	August – Oct.	Late summer/autumn bedding
Aster Single	March – April under glass	August – Oct.	Good late cut flower
Calendula Marigold	March – June outdoors; August – Sept. outdoors for early flowers next year	June – Oct.	Bright flowers for sunny borders or cutting
Candytuft	March – June outdoors; August – Sept. for next year	June – Sept.	Carpet or edging; sow frequently for succession
Canary Creeper Tropaeolum Canariense	April outdoors; March under glass	July – Sept.	Quick-growing yellow creeper
Chrysanthemum	March – May outdoors	July – Oct.	Good for late borders and cutting
Clarkia	March – May outdoors	July – Sept.	Graceful sunny border plant
Cornflower	March – June outdoors; August – Sept. for next year	June – Oct.	Tall border plant; ideal buttonhole flower
Cosmos	March – April under glass	July – Oct.	Handsome tall border plant and cut flower
Dianthus Baby Doll	April – May outdoors; Feb. – March under glass	July – Oct.	Pretty edging or carpet

	Sowing	Flowering	Notes
Godetia	March – June outdoors; August – Sept. for next year	June – Sept.	Neat habit like a dwarf shrub
Gypsophila Elegans	March – May outdoors; August – Sept. for next year	June – Sept.	Fine foil for other flowers and cutting
Helichrysum Strawflower	March – April under glass	August – Oct.	Cut and dry for winter flower arrangements
Larkspur	March – June outdoors; August – Sept. for next year	June – Sept.	Fine tall border plant
Linaria Fairy Bouquet	March – May outdoors; August – Sept. for next year	June – Sept.	Light, airy groundcover
Lobelia Pendula	March – April under glass	June – Oct.	Trailing plant for tubs or window boxes
Lobelia String of Pearls	Feb. – May under glass	June – Oct.	Under-planting, carpet or edging
Mesembryanthemum Criniflorum	March – April under glass	June – August	Carpet or edging in full sun
Mignonette Sweet Scented	March – April outdoors	June – Sept.	Sweet scented plants for half shade
Morning Glory Ipomea	March – April under glass	July – Sept.	Beautiful climber for a warm place
Nasturtium Dwarf	April – June outdoors	July – Oct.	Carpet or edging for dry soil
Nasturtium Giant Climbing	April – June outdoors	July – Oct.	Covers large area of ground or can be trained up fence or trellis

Name	Sowing	Flowering	Remarks
Annuals			
Nasturtium Gleam Hybrids	April – June outdoors	July – Oct.	Bright colour in poor soil
Nemesia	April – May outdoors; Feb. – March under glass	June – August	Pretty carpet and bedding plant
Nemophila Baby Blue Eyes	March – June outdoors; August – Sept. for next year	June – August	Pretty blue carpet
Nicotiana Tobacco Plant	March – April under glass	July – Oct.	Fine border plant; some varieties scented at night
Nigella Love-in-a-mist	March – June outdoors; August–Sept. for next year	June – Sept.	Pretty feathery plant for borders and cut flowers
Petunia	March – April under glass	June – Sept.	Ideal for bedding and window boxes
Phacelia Campanularia	March – June outdoors; August – Sept. for next year	June – Sept.	Pretty blue carpet for sunny beds
Phlox	March – April under glass	July – Sept.	Bedding, carpet and window boxes
Californian Poppy Eschscholzia	March – May outdoors; August – Sept. for next year	June – Sept.	Bright plant to fill gaps in sunny borders
Shirley Poppy	March – June outdoors; August – Sept. for next year	June – Sept.	Plant in large groups in the border

Name	Sowing	Flowering	Notes
Schizanthus Butterfly Flower	April – May outdoors; March – April under glass	June – Oct.	Easily grown exotic for the border
Statice	Feb. – March under glass	June – Sept.	Ideal to dry for winter arrangements
Night Scented Stock Matthiola bicornis	March – June outdoors	June – Sept.	Sweet scented; flowers open at dusk
Ten Week Stock	March – April under glass	June – August	Sweet scented bedding
Virginian Stock	March – June outdoors; August – Sept. for next year	June – Sept.	Good mixed with Night Scented Stock
Sunflower	March – May outdoors	July – Sept.	Spectacular height
Sweet Pea	March – May outdoors; Jan. – Feb. under glass or Sept. – Oct. in cold frame for next year	June – Sept.	Best-known annual climber
Sweet Scabious	April – May outdoors; Feb. – March under glass	July – Sept.	Good for border and cutting
Sweet Sultan	March – May outdoors	July – Sept.	Sunny border and for cutting
Verbena	March – April under glass	July – Sept.	Bedding and carpet plant for sunny position
Viscaria	March – May outdoors	June – Sept.	For borders and cutting
Zinnia	May outdoors; March under glass	August – Oct.	Rich colour for sunny borders